BURIED CITIES AND ANCIENT TREASURES

DORA JANE HAMBLIN

BURIED CITIES AND ANCIENT TREASURES

Illustrated with photographs

SIMON AND SCHUSTER   NEW YORK

76-6107

For Mary Jane, who was there

CONTENTS

PREFACE

Most Americans know little about the nation of Turkey, except perhaps the name of Ataturk, the expression "young Turks," and the fact that the whirling dervishes came from there. This is a pity, because the long peninsula at the eastern end of the Mediterranean, which is also often called Anatolia, played an exciting and colorful role in the drama of ancient culture which belongs to us all. Old Anatolia was a land bridge between the West, which was Europe, and the East of Persia, China, Mongolia. Here for centuries the marching armies of Alexander the Great and Genghis Khan, of Greeks and Romans and Trojans and Persians and nations now long dead and forgotten met each other and fought and intermingled. Furthermore, Anatolia/Turkey is intimately associated with a great number of people whom we know quite well—everybody from Santa Claus to Antony and Cleopatra, from King Croesus to the Virgin Mary.

This book is about those people, and about all those vanished nations which no one had ever heard about fifty years ago. It is about the exciting world of the archaeologists, who are bringing them back to life by digging out, from the debris of the centuries, the remains they left behind.

Three years ago in a book called *Pots and Robbers* I tried to write some of the adventures I had seen and heard about in Italy as archaeologists uncovered lost cities and battled with grave robbers and tourists for possession of the beautiful bits of antiquity that survive under the soil of Italy. *Pots and Robbers* was neither a textbook nor a comprehensive study. It was just a collection of stories I found too good not to be told, or in some cases retold.

Buried Cities and Ancient Treasures is a similar book, though it approaches some civilizations and cities that are less well known than those of Italy. Many of them are also far more exotic. This is not an expert's book; I am not an archaeologist. In some ways it is a travel journal, because in spite of all my reading, I had to discover the wonders of archaeology in Turkey by going there to see them.

Many people helped. I am indebted to Raci Temizer of the Archaeological Museum of Ankara, to Necati Dolunay and his assistant Miss Iyhan Birand of the Archaeological Museum of Istanbul, Mr. and Mrs. Guido Aliotti of Izmir, photographer Ara Guler and Perihan Kuterman of Istanbul, and American diver/archaeologists Peter Throckmorton of Athens and Dr. George Bass of the University of Pennsylvania. I shall be emotionally indebted forever to the generosity of Miss Theresa Goell and to Dr. Kenan Erim of New York City for having shared with me their fascinating finds at Nemrud Dagh and at Aphrodisias.

Associated Press correspondent Nick Luddington and Turkish journalist Mehmet Ali Kislali, both in Ankara, and journalist Dorothy Bacon in London were invaluable, as was that incorrigible amateur archaeologist in San Francisco, Mt. Ararat's own John Libi. I am grateful to Mary Jane Grunsfeld of Chicago, who shared the perils of the trip, did some of the interviews, and read the manuscript; to Marcia Weiner in New York, who suggested the book in the first place; and to Simonetta Toraldo in Rome, who typed it.

Perhaps I shall remember longest all those enchanting Turks whom I encountered along the way: the filling-station men offering Pepsi-Cola on hot days; the farmers who proffered apples and walnuts and free advice when I lost my way; Aziz the intrepid mountain man, Kenan the driver, Oral the interpreter; all those people who smiled as our lives touched, for a moment. The truth in this book comes from all the above people and their help. The errors, of fact or of judgment, are mine.

BURIED CITIES AND ANCIENT TREASURES

1

THE MOUND

We were jolting along in a red Ford which was about as far from its Detroit birthplace as it could get. Outside the windows were the gentle slopes of a range of mountains called the Anti-Taurus, in eastern Turkey, less than 500 miles from the border of the Soviet Union. The landscape was exotic and strangely quiet, as if both time and human beings had suddenly stopped, and were just standing there.

Off to the right, a flock of dirty white sheep munched at short grass and a solitary shepherd stood as still as stone, dressed from head to foot in a ragged sheepskin cloak. On the left, snuggled under an overhanging rock, was a cluster of black tents made from the skins of long-haired goats. They were nomad tents, the homes of a wandering group of Bedouin—tents strangely romantic to look at, probably miserable to live in.

Then we whirled through a village, throwing up clouds of brown dust which caked the outside of the car. The village houses were the same color as the dust, because in effect they were made from it: they were constructed of mud brick, dried in the sun, with flat roofs on which the families slept in summer when the nights were too hot for anyone to be inside. Down from each flat

On the road to Nemrud Dagh, in the eastern part of Turkey, we could see a mud-hut village through the windshield of our car.

roof to the street was a strange sloping ladder made of small logs, with no handrails for protection. The villagers walked as casually up and down these ladders as if they had been proper stairways.

Our Ford's Turkish driver, named Kenan, slouched well over into the left-hand corner of the front seat, driving with one hand. He was a city man who didn't much like the country, and he kept glancing gloomily at his rear-view mirror, from which dangled an assortment of good-luck charms. One of them looked startlingly like a bright blue eye embedded in a sickly-white eyeball. This particular charm was supposed to ward off the evil eye. Turkey is a nation of predominantly dark-haired and dark-eyed people, and Kenan, even though he himself had sandy hair and blue eyes, adhered to the prevailing belief that most of Turkey's troubles had come historically from foreign devils with blue eyes.

Kenan didn't in fact know what to make of us. I have blue eyes, but my companion in the back seat has brown eyes. We were foreigners, and female, and far from the path taken by most tourists to Turkey, but the only devilment we had caused up to then was to ask Kenan to take this horrible road to a village he had never heard of. He had already been lost three times, the radiator had boiled over twice, and the rear axle was developing an ominous clanking noise. But Kenan, like most Turks, had the resigned optimism of the Moslem religion. He shrugged and murmured an invocation to Allah. *"Mashallah,"* he said—"God willing, everything will be all right"—and on we went.

One of the wheels threw up a fist-sized boulder which smacked against the bottom of the back seat so hard that it actually hurt our feet. Kenan laughed for the first time, removed his right foot from the accelerator, and shook it sympathetically in the air.

By now we had left the villages behind. There was not a tree or shrub in sight, and no movement except for a quick scurry of black goats, those hardy animals which in this part of the world seem able to survive on nothing more nourishing than their own powerful smell. It was dusty and depressing. Kenan suddenly opened the glove compartment, extracted a small bottle, and passed it back to me. I thought it must be some mysterious Turkish potion to relieve depression, and I was about to take a sip of it when he snatched it out of my hands and applied it, liberally, to his face and hair. It was cologne, which I later learned is standard equipment in Turkish automobiles and taxis, carried to refresh the passengers and remove the dust.

Then we careened around one more curve and were on the top of a hill, and sweeping down and out in front was a long, majestic valley with at the end of it the thin glitttering line of a river.

"Firat su!" Kenan exclaimed, pointing.

"The Euphrates River," translated Kenan's companion in the front seat, an English-speaking Turk named Oral.

17

The mound of Samosata and the little modern town of Samsat, just to the right, lie in the Euphrates River valley.

I nearly jumped out of the car. The Euphrates River! When, I wondered, had I first heard that name: one of the rivers that flowed through ancient lands which had been "the cradle of civilization"? Many people first encounter it in Sunday school. It is mentioned in Genesis, Chapter 2: "A river flowed out of Eden to water the garden, and there it divided and became four rivers . . . and the name of the third river is Tigris . . . and the name of the fourth river is the Euphrates." (This quotation, and most of the others in the book, are from the Revised Standard Version of the Bible.)

In my case, I had learned the two names together. It was years before I found out that "Tigris-and-Euphrates" wasn't all one word.

From the top of our hill, the storied Euphrates didn't look nearly grand enough for its reputation. It was far away, of course, but even so it seemed small, lost in its broad shallow bed.

Then, suddenly, we saw the Mound. The Mound, a huge earthen structure, stood on the near bank of the Euphrates, 750 feet long from north to south, 450 feet across from east to west. It was stark, flat-topped, clearly man-made, and it sent shivers of excitement like splintering ice all through me. The Mound proved the grandeur of the little Euphrates, because once it had been a city, a series of cities, one piled on top of another. It proved that people had lived here, generation after generation, for thousands of years, on the banks of the life-giving river.

Mounds are of crucial importance in the study of human life because they are made from the debris, the wreckage, that ancient peoples left behind them. Nowhere on earth are they more numerous, or more important, than in the Middle East—the lands to the east of the Mediterranean Sea. There, in Turkey and Iran, in Iraq and Israel and Syria, the whole story of the beginnings of human community life and civilization lies hidden in the mounds.

The very building material of the Middle East, the sun-dried brick still used today, lent itself to mound-building because it was easy to work with but rather short-lived. Early city dwellers built their brick houses, sometimes on stone foundations, only to see them disintegrate slowly through the buffeting of wind and rain or to see them violently destroyed by bands of roaming marauders or neighbors looking for more territory. Each time the homes were destroyed, however, the villagers simply built them back up again, on top of the ruins. There was a strange tenacity about those ancient city dwellers: if a people's ancestors had lived in a certain place, the descendants tended to stay there, or to return there after wandering. No matter how many times the roof came down around their ears, no matter how many times enemies sacked the place, they returned. In each layer of habitation they abandoned broken kitchen utensils or weapons and covered up everything, and gradually through the years the city sites rose, a few inches or a few feet in a century. Some mounds

● Istanbul
  (Constantinople)

● Canakkale
  Hissarlik *(Troy)* 8

● Ankara
●*(Gordion)* 14

● Boghazkoy 6
  (Hattusas)
  (Yazilikaya)

● Bergama 7
  (Pergamum)

Athens

● Izmir   ● Sart 13
  (Smyrna)   *(Sardis)*

● Selçuk
  (Ephesus)
● Geyre 12   ● Burdur 11
  (Aphrodisias)   *(Hacilar)*

●Cumra 1, 9   ● Eregli 6
  (Çatal Hüyük)   *(Ivriz)*

Bodrum 13
● *(Halicarnassus)*

Tarsus 15
● *(Tarsus)*

Antakya ●
(Antioch)

TURKEY

Modern names are in roman type and the old names are in
italics. Arabic numbers indicate the chapters in which the
places are discussed.

are low, some are high, depending upon the terrain and the
length of time they were inhabited.

No mound in the Middle East could be more glorious, I
thought, could look more perfectly the way a mound *should* look,
than that one off on the horizon. That one, on the banks of the
Euphrates, had once been a city called Samosata, a city which a
hundred years before Christ was known throughout the ancient
world. Its position was strategic, on the banks of the great river
and on the crossroads for the camel-caravan routes of the day.
From here, resupplied with water, the caravans came and went in
four directions: north to the Black Sea and the Caucasus; south
to powerful ancient Egypt and her Pharaohs; east to Palestine
and, beyond, to China; west to Athens, to Sparta, to Rome.

Even Kenan was impressed. He headed the car down the long
hill, going slowly, and excitedly he asked Oral who had built the
mound and why. We coasted slowly toward it, and at the nearest
point on the road, in a small village, we stopped. Instantly the
car was surrounded. Tall, thin men with three-day beards and
flat, billed caps put their faces almost against the glass of the

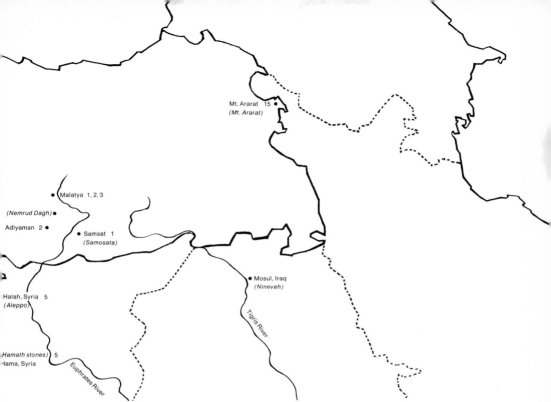

windows. Dirty children with wild hair and beautiful eyes crowded through the men's legs. Scrawny dogs were kicked away, yelping, by dirty bare feet. Passing women hurriedly pulled their head scarves across their faces, holding the scarf ends in their teeth, in the old-fashioned Middle Eastern gesture to cover the face in public. Some of the women carried bundles of twigs on their heads, or jars of water, and all walked with a sloping, graceful slouch.

Beside almost every house was a neat pile of animal dung to be used for fuel, worked into shapes that looked like circular bricks. Each pile was stacked up around a stick which held the mass together. The houses were tumbling-down mud brick, with here and there the startling white gleam of a shaped and beautiful stone holding up a crazily tilting roof or a sagging corner. Ancient Samosata had clearly come down in the world. The old city lay hidden in the Mound, and at its feet was this ragtag town which still kept a version of the old name: it was called Samsat.

Suddenly the children started to point at our little group and chant something that sounded like "Meezgole, Meezgole."

21

"What are they saying?" we asked Oral.

"I have no idea," he confessed. "It is not a word I know."

Then we got out of the car, and the children went into a frenzy of glee, setting up such a hullabaloo that they brought a neat, thin man with a trimmed black mustache hurrying to the car. Despite two inches of dust underfoot and a blazing sun overhead, the man had on a shirt so clean that it gleamed, and spotless white trousers with a thin black stripe. When he smiled, his teeth were as white as his shirt. Could he, he asked in polite Turkish, be of assistance?

"The ladies," said Oral, "would like to see the Mound."

Aziz—for his name proved to be Aziz—spoke no language that we ladies could understand, but he inclined his head with the pleased dignity of an overtipped headwaiter. But of course, he indicated. He, Aziz, was a member of the archaeological expedition even now working on the mound, and he would be delighted to show us around.

Kenan, who was beginning to think that archaeology might be interesting, decided to go with us. He locked the car and threatened the swarm of children with lumps and bruises if they so much as touched a fender. We all set forth, perspiring under a wickedly hot blue sky, across the leafless plain. The nearer we got, the higher the mound looked—150, 160 feet, almost straight up. Under our feet were bits of broken stone, pebbles, occasionally a fragment of pottery, a broken piece that archaeologists call a "potsherd" or just a "sherd." Aziz stopped and touched one piece gently with the toe of his shoe. "This is three thousand, maybe four thousand years old," he explained quietly to Oral. "We find a lot of it."

On top of the mound was some crumbling masonry, perhaps the remnants of a defensive wall. Through Oral, we asked Aziz about it, and he shrugged. Not very important, he said; in fact, quite recent by the standards of this ancient land. Probably it had been built no more than a thousand years ago, by the Crusaders on one of their many campaigns toward Jerusalem.

The way up was a steep switchback trail cut into the mound's side by the archaeologists, and when we arrived puffing and panting at the top, there was a magnificent view up and down the valley of the Euphrates. The entire countryside looked barren, abandoned. Could this landscape have been part of the cradle of civilization? History says that it was. Once perhaps it had been forested and lush, but then early men discovered agriculture, and domesticated animals, and cut trees for fires, and in the process they wore out the land and grazed it to death and denuded the hills.

Yet once across these valleys and hills marched armies of Greeks and Persians, battling each other for control of the river and the fortified cities. Right down there, on the banks of the Euphrates, two thousand years ago the Roman legions, having marched all the way across Italy, Yugoslavia, Greece and Bulgaria and half the width of modern Turkey, had met the soldiers of a nation called Parthia which once ruled the territory that is to-day's northwestern Iran. They were fighting, as usual, for control of this key riverside stronghold. Because the Romans were on one side of the river and the Parthians on the other, they had some difficulty getting at each other. But their confrontation so long ago still lives in our speech in the phrase "Parthian shot," which originally meant a rearward shot by a fleeing mounted archer. It has come to mean any sharp parting remark, and we have cor-rupted it from "Parthian shot" to "parting shot."

The most dramatic sight of all from the top of the mound was a mountain 34 miles away with a perfect cone on its top, dark blue against the light blue sky.

"Nemrud Dagh," said Aziz, pointing. In English the words mean simply Nemrud (or Nimrod) mountain, but the Turkish name seems to me far more romantic. On top of Nemrud Dagh is one of the world's most incredible monuments: a collection of statues of gods erected in honor of himself by a certain King Antiochus who ruled a very small independent kingdom in the first century before Christ. On Nemrud Dagh was his memorial, and the city of Samosata, buried in the Mound on which we stood, was his capital. From where we were we could see Anti-ochus' whole little kingdom, though we could not know for sure just who were the people he ruled or where they had come from. His kingdom was called Commagene, and little is known about it except that the Greek geographer/historian Strabo (about 63

B.C.–A.D. 24) called Commagene "an exceedingly fertile, though small, territory." There also are historical records that about the year 64 B.C. King Antiochus made a treaty with the Roman general Pompey, possibly to avoid being conquered, and took his kingdom voluntarily into the embrace of the Roman Empire.

As the centuries passed, however, the world forgot about little Commagene and a king called Antiochus. Classical scholars knew about them, but actually even these men knew little more than that such a person and such a kingdom had existed. Antiochus, his mountain, and his mound have come back to life only through the exertions of present-day archaeologists.

That day we watched the native diggers using light, long-handled shovels to toss away dirt and debris from a series of low walls. They were exposing a Turkish city that dated from about A.D. 1000, a city that must have stood there when the Crusaders built their big walls around the edge of the mound. Halfway down the side, another knot of diggers was carefully clearing some black-and-white mosaic floors dating from the Byzantine Empire about A.D. 500. Below that, when they get down to it, they expect to find remains of Antiochus' city. And below that . . . well, somebody's hands four thousand years ago must have fashioned the pottery that broke and lies in fragments down below, at the foot of the mound.

Thoroughly excavating and exploring a mound like this one destroys it, in the end. Archaeologists simply reverse the mound-building process by starting at the top and working carefully downward—removing layer after layer of debris and buildings, sifting the soil for fragments, measuring and photographing and analyzing as they go. Britain's Seton Lloyd, one of the most experienced of mound excavators, once wrote ruefully (in *Mounds of the Near East*, Aldine Publishing Company, Chicago) that "in a Near Eastern mound, the end product [of an archaeological exploration] is often a deep hole in the ground. . . ."

It is also, with luck, one more interlocking chapter in the slowly unfolding story of men and women who lived on earth in days past our remembering.

I looked down at my feet, all but buried in the dust on top of the mound, and wondered what the archaeologists would find,

Turkish diggers working at three different levels on the mound have just exposed the Byantine paving (center left).

At the foot of the mound, the diggers cut a bit of Roman mosaic paving so that it can be removed to a museum for safekeeping.

eventually, of Antiochus' town. Would it really be there? Had Antiochus really existed? And what about King Midas, he of the "golden touch," or King Croesus, who was so rich that we still today say "rich as Croesus"? These kings, according to legend, lived in what is now Turkey. The "Gordian knot" was in Turkey too—that fancy bit of rope-tying which no sovereign in ancient times could undo. We still use the phrase in English, to represent a knotty problem. A town that may have been the first real city, built more than 8,000 years ago, is in Turkey at a place called Çatal Hüyük. And off there to the east, not visible from the mound, is a mountain called Ararat, where Noah's Ark was reputed to have come to rest. All these myths, all these legends, are proving, one by one, to be true under the picks and shovels of the archaeologists in Turkey.

While I was brooding about all this, there suddenly materialized before me a young man with a beard and a turned-up Australian-style hat and a strong American accent.

"Hi," he said. "I'm Jonathan. My aunt is in charge of this dig. Won't you come down to the expedition house and have some tea? I'll show you our treasures, and our Roman wall."

At the foot of the hill we were again joined by most of the population of Samsat. This time, however, awed by the presence of Jonathan and Aziz, they didn't crowd or shout. They simply walked along with us, silent and wide-eyed, like an honor guard.

"Sorry about them," said Jonathan. "I'm afraid we are, at the moment, the only road show in town. They don't have much to look at, and we are it."

He led the way to a long section of rock wall, on the edge of town. It had been built by Roman soldiers, those indomitable rock cutters who were trained, between battles, to hack out rock and turn it into roads, aqueducts, bridges. That old wall no doubt helped establish the present location of the village of Samsat, because its carefully fitted stones were just standing there waiting to be used again. The shaped whitish stones I had seen earlier, propping up the mud-brick houses, had been cut by the Romans. In the summer of 1970 the Samosata archaeological expedition, in addition to working on the mound, had cleared several yards of the old wall, dug out a circular building which might have been either a public bath or some kind of shrine, and then hit upon the sort of junk heap only an archaeologist can love —an abandoned cistern into which somebody had tossed broken pottery, the tops of columns, all manner of discarded household objects. The inhabitants of Samsat had looked on with amazement as the "crazy foreigners" lovingly salvaged all this old junk and carried it away.

The "junk" went, together with all the bits found on the mound, into the expedition house, a low, mud-brick, but notably clean peasant house rented for the season. Jonathan and his aunt and Aziz had struggled to make it civilized, putting up lengths of cloth as a screen against sun and dust. They had painted the dried mud walls, and they were nursing some scrawny plants in a small, high-fenced garden. Also in the garden were wooden boxes, cardboard boxes, baskets, all filled with bits of broken pottery or half-assembled clay and stone figures, neatly numbered.

Inside the Spartan expedition headquarters there was neither running water nor electricity, but under every bed, behind each flimsy door, on a dozen rickety shelves were treasures. There were ancient oil lamps; there were fragments of carved inscriptions left by a mysterious people called the Hittites, whose very existence had been forgotten until fifty years ago. There were very old vases with ingenious "strainers" made of perforated pottery in their necks. There were the carved capitals of marble columns, and a thick flat stone upon which some apprentice mason had, two thousand years ago, practiced drilling holes of various sizes.

More than anything else, there was proof that once upon a time the presence of strangers and foreigners was an everyday occurrence in this old city by the river: there was pottery of Chinese origin, there were Greek pieces, there was Persian ware. All came from the days of the camel caravans, when Samosata was better known than London and Paris, 1,500 years before America was even discovered.

Jonathan, prancing from one small shelf to another to show us the best pieces, was growing eloquent about the pleasures of gluing pots back together again. "It's an addictive thing, like eating sunflower seeds," he said. His speech was interrupted by a loud banging at the front gate and a breathless messenger from the town's only telephone. Jonathan's aunt had just called, said the messenger, to report that she could not come back to the expedition house that night. She had been told that there were two foreign ladies there. She had no idea who they were, but she would be pleased if they would join her that evening for dinner in the nearest large village, Adiyaman. She would like Aziz to accompany them, and she would await the party in the town square at 6 P.M.

Reluctantly, Jonathan escorted us back to the car. It would have been nice, he said, to spend the evening with someone from home, to speak English and relax. As we got back into the Ford, the children set up their chant of "Meezgole, Meezgole," and this time Oral the interpreter could stand it no longer.

"What does that mean?" he asked Jonathan and Aziz, and both of them laughed.

"My aunt is Miss Theresa Goell," said Jonathan. "In this village the children think that 'Miss Goell' means 'foreign lady.'"

2

THE DIGGER

The real Meezgole was standing in the deep dusk of a Turkish twilight in the main square of the town of Adiyaman, peering at the passing scene through very thick glasses. There wasn't a great deal to peer at: two parked jeeps, which looked as if they had survived the World War II battle of El Alamein, but only just; a thin procession of loaded donkeys, each attended by its baggy-pantalooned master; two competing ramshackle hotels facing each other across the square like gun fighters in a cowboy movie. Miss Goell, who knows the territory, was standing discreetly on neutral ground between hotels. If her visitors hadn't chosen one yet, she wasn't going to be responsible for influencing their decision. No matter which one they went to, the owner of the other would be furious.

Miss Goell was done up in a brown-and-white print dress, brown-and-white openwork shoes, and a big, floppy white straw hat with a band of the same material as the dress. But her crowning glory was a Phi Beta Kappa key, firmly affixed over the bosom on the left. There were at the most only four living souls in all of Adiyaman that night who could possibly have recognized this symbol of her academic achievements, but they all got the full

The main square of Adiyaman where we met "Meezgole," the archaeologist Theresa Goell. The ruins at left are from natural collapse, not war damage.

effect of it: Miss Goell herself, the two of us, and the Turkish governor of the province, for whom she had worn the key in the first place. The chief point of her trip to Adiyaman was to confer with the governor about protection and storage of the treasures from the Mound, and she had dressed up out of respect both for her position and for his.

"How nice of you to have come all this way!" she exclaimed. "Now, go and have a wash—heavens, I hope there's water. We will dine over there," she added, gesturing vaguely toward a dark blur on the other side of the square.

The restaurant she had chosen turned out to be a latticework afterthought perched precariously on the roof of a sagging building, but its beaming proprietor recognized the lady archaeologist and rushed forward to greet her with enthusiasm. He also provided spectacularly fast service: at his very best table, he grabbed up the soiled plates from the previous diners and polished them forthwith on a grimy towel that dangled from his belt. Then he put the shining plates down again, neatly, and bellowed for waiters.

Miss Goell arranged the seating, ordered the food, and talked about her work. She is that classic romantic figure, the field archaeologist, "the digger." Few professions in the world sound so glamorous and exciting to the outsider, and few are so grindingly difficult for the practitioner. She and Jonathan and the faithful Aziz and a Turkish archaeologist had been at their lonely work on the Mound for two months. For two months they had worked sixteen-hour days, taken baths out of a bucket, and lived on often appalling food.

"We are up at four-thirty A.M. and try to be on the mound by five-thirty, because of the heat," she explained. "In August and early September the temperature at the top is a hundred and thirty degrees at midday. Very debilitating. By late September it seldom gets to more than a hundred and twenty. We stop work at four-thirty in the afternoon, but then there's all the classifying to do, and cataloguing of our finds, and the photography. And there are complications with the digging crew. Samsat is a very poor village—rather a desperate one, really. There must be six hundred men who want work, so we try to rotate the jobs. We pay about a dollar twenty-five a day, which is good pay here. But trying to divide the work among all who want it does complicate our bookkeeping, and also the morning line-up for the march to the Mound."

As she described the job-sharing and the job itself, I kept remembering the first time I had met her, almost a year before, in my apartment in New York. I had heard of her work, and impulsively I telephoned her just to ask about it. Just as impulsively, she decided to come see me and talk about it. It was one of those cold, blustery New York nights when a perverse wind insisted upon blowing smoke from my fireplace back into the room, and "Meezgole" had cheerily coughed and spluttered and remarked that it was "Just like Turkey—either you're being roasted alive or else it's cold and the wood won't burn. But I love Turkey. The people, the villagers, are often so poor it makes you weep, but they have a simpleness, a sweetness . . ."

That night in New York I had thought she was telling a good story, trying to make it all more amusing to me. Now, several thousand miles from my apartment, eating tough shish-kebab from an almost-clean plate, remembering the dirty children and the dark lean men with their shovels, I was beginning to get a glimpse of the real life of a digger. It is a peculiar irony of archaeology that the people who practice it, who spend their lives digging up remnants of glorious past civilizations, must often do their work in geographical areas from which the comforts of civilization have long since departed.

No two archaeologists are exactly alike, of course, but Theresa Goell belongs to that small elite band who are willing to go anywhere, to put up with anything. Her age is a secret, but she graduated from Radcliffe College in 1923. She is a woman of immense scholarship, no nonsense, and lively humor. She also seems indestructible, which helps. She gets her kicks from the delirium of discovery and from the unpredictability of every day.

"If things get difficult in Samsat, I just go out in the moonlight and stroll beside 'my' Roman wall," she was saying over coffee in the restaurant. "You can think long thoughts in the moonlight by a Roman wall. When you comprehend that the Romans walked all that way, all the way to central Turkey, and they left behind a few potsherds, and walls, and bridges, and after they left the people went right back to their old lives, as if the Romans had never been . . ."

Like many another lady, Miss Goell found the love of her life in a strange place: standing in line in Greenwich Village waiting to vote. Near her in line was a man who began to talk about a mountain called Nemrud Dagh. It was 7,000 feet high, he told her, remote, pelted by hail and battered by wind. On top of it, carved out of the living stone, were giant heads and long inscriptions in Greek. Miss Goell's informant was a New York University professor who was not an archaeologist but who had heard of the mountain from friends. He told her it had first been noted in modern times by a wandering German engineer who climbed the peak in 1880 and went home babbling about "heads twenty feet high." Few people believed him, but within five years both a German expedition and a Turkish one had struggled to the top of Nemrud Dagh. They said that the heads and the inscriptions were there, all right, but the sculpture seemed "neither Greek nor Roman," so they weren't much interested. In the late nineteenth century, archaeological interest centered around Egypt and Greece and Rome; other periods and other cultures were too little known. So Antiochus and his mountain and his mound slept on, undisturbed.

To Theresa Goell, however, the mysterious mountain seemed "halfway between earth and heaven," and she determined to see it. It was eight years before she did. World War II intervened, and her own studies, and the need for funds for the trip. Finally, in 1947, she made it—but it wasn't easy.

"Nobody seemed to know for sure just which town Nemrud Dagh was nearest to, or how to get there," she said. "I started out from Tarsus, in southeastern Turkey, by train and got as far as Golbasi, about two hundred miles away. There I hired a Turkish boy to carry my camping equipment, and we sort of played it by ear. We rode on a decrepit truck all one night to get here, to Adiyaman. The trucks went only at night because of the terrible heat of the daytime. Our particular truck should have been decently laid to rest twenty years before we rode it, but it got us here."

She waved her arms around in the darkness of Adiyaman in 1970 and described how it had looked such a short time ago as 1947: "Our poor truck was the only one in town, that time. Most travel was still by camel caravan, as it must have been in Antiochus' time. All night long tethered donkeys brayed in the courtyard there, and before dawn the camel caravans moved out with their peculiar majesty. They're actually nasty beasts, camels. . . ."

She and her Turkish boy went off several times in the wrong direction, misguided by natives who had never been to Nemrud Dagh. They walked, they camped, they rode donkeys and mules. "You can walk for miles, you know, holding on to the tail of a mule," Miss Goell observed. "Finally we found the mountain, and we climbed it, and I was overwhelmed. The heads, those magnificent heads. I knew this place would be my life's work."

In 1953 she led her first expedition up the rocky slopes, and the experience turned out to be a short course in survival techniques. Field archaeology is never simple: Professor George M. A. Hanfmann of Harvard, working at another Turkish site in 1961, talked of "donkeys, sheep, and horses that invade the camp . . . Trucks rumble all night depositing bricks for construction. . . . Howling jackals join the concert. . . . The horse-drawn water cart falls into a pit, leaving shrieking staff members high and dry in the showers as the water gives out. . . ."

Such problems would have been luxuries on top of Nemrud Dagh, that first season.

"We had to camp on top of the mountain to do our work, to survey the site," Theresa Goell explains. "The nearest village was straight down, an hour and a half away. There was no water on the mountain, not even one tree for shade or wood. The wind never stopped blowing. Our tents were so battered we finally built six-foot-high walls of loose stone around them for protection."

Every sip of water, every scrap of food, every piece of firewood had to be hauled up the mountain by donkey or muleback, and the expedition postman had to make a two-day journey to dispatch or pick up mail. Daytime temperatures in summer were 130 degrees, but nighttime was near freezing. Then there were the wolves, and the bears.

Still the expedition members persevered, year after year, sponsored by the National Geographic Society, the American Schools of Oriental Research, the Bollingen Foundation, the American Philosophical Society, and private patrons like Mr. and Mrs. Philip Godfrey.

"Some seasons I spent alone up there with six or seven Kurdish shepherds. We all slept in one tent for protection, with a man on guard all night to deal with the wolves and the bears." Miss Goell now was speaking quietly, reminiscently, and Aziz was nodding his head in the candlelight of the Adiyaman restaurant. Was it he, I wondered, who had stayed up all night, watching the fire and holding the rifle? He spoke suddenly, rapidly, to the interpreter, who relayed his words to us.

"The bears, they come and dig for roots. Every year we would come back to the excavation site and find holes, holes everywhere. Meezgole, she always said, 'Who has been digging here?' But it was always the bears, looking for food. The wolves, they are different. They jump mostly in the settlements, in the corrals, and take the animals."

Meezgole broke in again. "I think they sometimes ate better than we did," she said, "although the men were wonderful. In summer they found cucumbers, tomatoes, a lot of gourds, eggplant. The Kurds make eggplant with chopped chicken meat. Most of the meat here is like spring steel, but you can always grind it up and swallow it in small bits. Sometimes they would kill a young goat in the village and bring it up, and then we would have a feast."

When they weren't battling to live, the diggers dug. On the summit of Nemrud Dagh was an open-air temple containing a sculptured collection of all the gods worshiped by the pagan king Antiochus. He claimed descent on his father's side from Persian rulers and on his mother's side from the Macedonian Alexander the Great, so he was careful to be polite to the gods of both civilizations. His workmen had carved broad terraces out of the rock at the top of the mountain and erected there the images of the gods. Antiochus, who considered himself also a god, chose to be depicted in 18 feet of solid rock as a young man with rather Greek features but with a Persian headdress, honoring his father's side of the family.

Carefully, Miss Goell's Kurdish shepherds removed 20 feet of debris from the sprawling terrace on the eastern side of the mountaintop, and carried it down the slopes on improvised litters because there was no place to dump it on top. Between the statues and the other terraces they found a cone almost 150 feet high, built into perfect symmetry perhaps by Antiochus' carvers who threw their scraps of rock there as they fell off in the carving.

One day early in the digging, workmen came upon the head of a man, lying face up toward the sky. The head was 18 feet tall, and weighed three tons. As its stone features emerged, little by little, even the workmen were awed.

"One of them said to me, 'This god has been sleeping here for two thousand years, and now we have disturbed him! Something terrible is going to happen,' " Miss Goell remembered.

Piously, they covered his unearthed face with a sheet. But that night so fierce a thunderstorm broke upon the mountain that the deluge almost washed the whole expedition back down the slopes to the Euphrates River.

"We were all," said Miss Goell, "a little reflective, next morning."

Part of her preoccupation, throughout the digging, must have come from her strange position: a foreign woman, alone with a work crew, probing on a mountain which the local inhabitants either feared or ignored. What was she looking for? Why was she there? Always, in Turkey, there are rumors of buried treasure, of gold. But no gold turned up on Nemrud Dagh: only the heads, and inscriptions the native diggers couldn't read. Miss Goell deciphered them, and read them aloud: "I, Antiochus I, King of Commagene, have raised this shrine on the topmost ridge of my kingdom . . . in closest proximity to the heavenly throne of . . . Zeus."

The Kurdish shepherds, mostly Moslems, murmured an invocation to their own god, Allah, and kept on digging.

Inevitably, Miss Goell became a missionary figure dispensing a daily wage, wisdom, medicine. She also became a court of appeals and a confidante of the workmen's wives: "I heard all about their troubles at home, their miscarriages, the illnesses of their children. The men talked of their troubles too, the struggle they have to buy even one animal, to live through the winter. They have the most appalling accidents. They can be almost scalped falling from rocks while tending their flocks. Or they get kicked in the face by a mule. Then, half dead, they struggle to me. I do what I can; I had a couple of first-aid courses during the war. But I keep thinking I'll be arrested for practicing medicine without a license."

It was growing late in Adiyaman, and as we rose to go home, Aziz made his longest speech of the evening.

"Meezgole, she has the roar of a lion sometimes, but her heart is pure," he said through the interpreter. "She is a friend to us and to Turkey. Do you know what happened one day on Nemrud Dagh? I'll tell you. The stupid people were asking again, 'What is the foreign lady doing on our mountain? Is she looking for gold?' And one of the men—one of the simple men, a digger—he turned on the stupid people and he said, 'No, she is only digging for our history.' "

Meezgole's eyes grew warm as she listened to this familiar story again, and then as we picked our way slowly in the dark out of the restaurant and back to the square, she announced firmly, "You will go to Nemrud Dagh tomorrow morning. Aziz will go with you."

3

MAROONED ON A MULE

Achieving this magic mountain, it turned out, involved several days of rising at 4:30 A.M.—a chore made somewhat less painful by the discomfort of most of the hotels within reachable distance. After five or six hours of examining the dubious mattresses and the even more dubious door locks, listening to dogfights in the street and encountering wandering, pajama-clad men in the hallways, any fool would conclude that he had had a good night's "rest" and would be willing to be up and about. The plumbing is perhaps the worst hazard. In this part of Turkey it is relentlessly unisex, primitively slippery underfoot, and overpoweringly smelly. I dealt with the dilemma by postponing it as long as possible and then holding my breath. My companion explained enigmatically that she dealt with it by "holding everything else."

At 5 A.M. we assembled in the square, shivering: Kenan the driver, Oral the interpreter, Aziz the faithful, the two of us, and, all of a sudden, a Turkish archaeologist from Samsat. Though he had grown up in this region, he, like most Turks, had never climbed Nemrud Dagh. His name turned out to be Nizamettin, but we all, suspecting he might have joined the group to keep us from tampering with the treasures, called him "Commissar." He was not in the least annoyed. The red Ford endured another hour of torture on the rocky roads, and then we stopped for breakfast in a garden at the town of Kahta. Turkish breakfast is different, but delicious: tea in glasses far too hot to handle until one has drunk enough of it to anesthetize the finger tips, bread, black olives, white cheese, and canned marmalade. The garden had a collection of scrawny trees, and strung from limb to limb were colored lights. Strolling under our feet and through the pathetic greenery were small fowl which looked like guinea hens done by Dali.

From Kahta the narrow road begins to climb toward Eski Kahta, which means in Turkish "old Kahta"—the ancient city. The tiny blue peak of Nemrud Dagh was visible all the way, though it never seemed to grow closer. We passed the mighty mound called Karakus, the burial place of Antiochus' womenfolk who weren't considered grand enough for the top of the mountain, and then the road wound itself into a coiled spring and twanged open, with us on it, into a great sweeping valley. A rocky gorge dominated the valley, and over it was a perfectly preserved Roman bridge, the only crossing even today over that part of the river Kahta, in ancient times called the Nymphaios. A single arch, perfectly proportioned, seemed almost to dance across the river, its whitish stone as sturdy as when it was built almost two thousand years ago. It was built in the time of the Roman emperor Septimius Severus, one of the nearly incredible travelers of his time: he was born in Leptis Magna, in North Africa, and he died a world away, in York, in England. In his era these far-flung places were all part of the Roman Empire, and it was the men of occupying Roman legions in Turkey who built that bridge in his honor on the route to Commagene and Samosata. Once it had four tall columns guarding the approaches; now there are only three. The fourth was taken down, legend says, when Septimius Severus' son Caracalla (he of the great baths in Rome, now used for summer opera) murdered his brother, Geta.

I kept turning back, to look at that bridge, until it vanished around a final curve, and there in front of us was Eski Kahta, with the towering, dramatic ruins of an Islamic fortress, six hun-

A Roman bridge on the road toward Eski Kahta, still in use by automobiles today, was erected by Roman legions as a monument to Septimius Severus.

dred years old, still dominating the tiny village of stone and mud houses. It was only 8:45 A.M., but my mind was already stuffed with a whole day's impressions, and when a pantalooned and snaggle-toothed village lady asked me for a cigarette, I wondered, bemused, where she had picked up that particular habit.

From Eski Kahta, the assault on Nemrud Dagh is on foot—your own or a mule's. It would be four or five hours up, everyone had said, only about three hours coming down. Oral, Aziz, and a villainous-looking man with a bandage over one eye were engaged in a shouting match which turned out to be the haggling over prices. Each mule, for the round trip, would cost 40 Turkish lire, then about $3. I was appalled to discover that there was no charge for the men who led the mules. Then it developed that Kenan the driver, whose longing to see the mountain had increased with every mile of the journey, didn't feel he could afford 40 lire for the trip. Hurried conference: we would pay for his mule. He had a look of great strength, Kenan did, and it occurred to me that even a mule might need a push, in the steep bits. Within moments six mules, their owners, and half the women and children in the village were out to see the triumphal departure. Aziz assigned the passengers to the mules. I got a rather tall, gray one, for which I was grateful because I always feel too big for regulation-size mules, donkeys, rickshas, and the like. My intrepid beast led the procession, being led itself by a tall old gentleman with white hair, tennis shoes, and an enormous rent in the right rear pantleg of his baggy trousers. We started straight down, over a rocky hillside, and across a narrow, crumbling stone bridge so steeply arched that I shut my eyes in sheer terror.

There is nothing to hold on to on a mule—just a great padded sort of saddle with no pommel and no stirrups and a general feeling of insecurity. I felt fragile as an egg balanced on a knife, and for the first hour I dared not move even my eyes for fear I'd fall off. I would recognize that mule's ears, and the rent in the leader's trousers, in a dim light anywhere in the world.

From behind I could hear the cries of the other drivers. *Hup!* they kept saying, and something that sounded like *Kootch!* and every now and then a distinct *Yahooo!* from Kenan, who turned

We rode to the top of the mound while the muleteers walked.

out to have the instincts of a cowboy even though, when we started out, he did manage to get on his mule on one side and promptly fall off the other.

Once past the bridge, we went up a stream. Not beside it—*in* it, with the drivers leaping delicately from rock to rock and the mules plodding along placidly. It made my feet hurt just to watch, so I began to look around. Nemrud Dagh itself was hidden, somewhere behind a cliff, but the scenery was magnificent. Scattered rocks, cliffs, sudden sharp valleys, twisted trees, and then a little village clinging like lichen to a mountainside, its houses the same color as the rock and earth they stood on. This was the village of Horuk, halfway up, and despite its height it looked oddly flat. For a moment I couldn't think why, and then I realized: there are no church spires in remote Turkish villages, or electric-light poles, or water towers: nothing to break the line. In the cities there are wonderful minarets—tall, thin towers from which the Moslems hear the daily calls to prayer—but in the small villages there are no minarets.

Horuk had a deep pure well, the last water before the summit of Nemrud Dagh, and grave-eyed village women handed up metal bowls of it for the riders to drink. Two other women were seated under a huge tree, with their children playing near them, weaving a long, long panel of bright cloth. I raised my camera and they jumped up and ran.

From muleback, the ruined ancient bridge seemed very steep.

The village of Horuk, where we stopped for water and lunch.

Horuk had only five houses and few animals when Theresa Goell began working on Nemrud Dagh. She hired its men as muleteers and diggers, and today the village has more than doubled in size. Miss Goell is, clearly, its patron saint. Aziz murmured something about "Meezgole," and a tall man with a uniform cap rushed from a neat doorway to invite us in. This was the guard of Nemrud Dagh, and he led us into a big, square room with layer upon layer of carpets on its beaten-earth floor. There were broad shelves at either end of the room, cushions scattered about, and we left our shoes outside. The idea was that we should sit down. I wouldn't have believed how difficult that simple operation is after two hours on a mule.

Among the reams of eager advice we had received about an

assault upon Nemrud Dagh was that we should be sure to carry along water, and nuts and raisins to eat. We had inadvertently abandoned the water jug at Eski Kahta, but we certainly did have nuts and raisins. We still had them two weeks later, as a matter of fact, my companion having bought enough for an attempt on Mt. Everest itself. At Horuk we produced the first of several dozen sacks of nuts, the mule drivers joined us, and we gravely munched and drank water and smiled at each other for fifteen minutes. I assumed this was lunch. I was wrong. In came piles of flat, unleavened bread; bowls of yoghurt; cheese; olives; omelettes; and heaps of grapes. For friends of Meezgole the village would provide.

After lunch, Nemrud Dagh was briefly visible as we rode. It didn't look one bit nearer than it had that morning in Kahta, but it was visible. By now Kenan and the Commissar were both riding sidesaddle, to ease their legs and to demonstrate their virtuosity on muleback, and I had achieved a sack-of-flour slouch which no doubt looked awful but felt fairly comfortable. This state of bliss lasted exactly forty-five minutes. Then the trail ended at the bottom of what appeared to be a nearly perpendicular hill of soft, slippery dirt. Everybody was instructed here to get down and walk. Everybody except me, that is. Before I had quite decided whether to fall off my mule to the left or to the right, my leader gave a mighty tug on the mule's rope, bellowed something loud, and started up the precipice dragging the mule behind him. I grabbed the front of the saddle and said politely, "No, no, I'd really prefer to walk with the others." No effect. "Uhhh, sir . . . ," tentatively. No response. Abandoning the ladylike approach, I wrenched around in the saddle and screamed, loudly, for Oral. "Tell this man I want to walk. *Walk!* How do you say 'walk'?" Why is it one never has a phrase book when it is really crucial? Oral didn't hear. That did it. I was marooned on a mule, out of communication with the world, headed straight up. I don't recall saying anything more, but it is possible that I moaned a bit. Aziz, who had remounted and now all but galloped past me (he doesn't weigh very much), mistook my moans of anguish for happy cries of joy and shouted, "Good mule!" as he went by. "*Walk; I want to walk!*" I shrieked again. "Good mule!"

47

repeated Aziz. These were, I discovered later, two of his five words of English. I liked all the other words better.

Finally we did walk, or scramble on all fours, up the last 50 yards of the steep slope and onto the West Terrace of Antiochus' great monument. Man-made, hacked like a shelf out of the mountain's living rock, the terrace was covered with topsy-turvy heads like some gigantic sculptor's studio left in disarray. The huge beaked stone head of a guardian eagle stood beside an Apollo whose nose had been broken off. Apollo's head was taller than a man, and behind it, leaning crazily as they had tumbled over, were great gray blocks of stone on which were carved reliefs of King Antiochus shaking hands and being greeted by deities of his day.

At the southern end of the terrace was an enormous slab of stone with a high relief of a lion, Hellenistic in style, bearing a six-pointed star on his flank and a crescent moon on his chest. This is the now-famous "lion horoscope," actually seen and described by the first Western expedition to climb the holy mountain in 1882, and it became known to archaeologists as the first Greek horoscope ever found. In the 1950s, Theresa Goell's expedition found another one, more fragmentary, on the East Terrace. From photographs, casts, and careful descriptions of these pre-Christian horoscopes, Professor Otto Neugebauer of Brown University has deciphered their meaning, or part of it. Some nineteen stars are scattered on or near the lion's body, and there is a conjunction of the planets Jupiter, Mercury, and Mars. The stars and the planets, read carefully, indicate to Professor Neugebauer the date of July 7, either 62 or 61 B.C. What could have been so important about this date to Antiochus? He ruled in Commagene from about 69 to 34 B.C., and archaeologists know from the translation of inscriptions on the site that Antiochus was born on January 16 and was crowned king on July 10, though they do not yet know in which years. The king left money and provided priests and musicians with orders to celebrate "everlasting" ceremonies on those two days of every year. The July 7 dating of the horoscope would indicate that it commemorates some event connected with his coronation rather than with his birth, and the best guess at the moment is that perhaps it marks his peace with

On top of Nemrud Dagh are these giant heads of ancient kings and gods.

the invading Romans and their confirmation of his right to rule Commagene. It seems odd that a man of the colossal pride of Antiochus, who converted an entire mountaintop to a celebration of himself and his "glorious ancestors," would commemorate a compromise, but perhaps he considered it an honor to be an ally of Rome.

To the left as we faced the tumbled majesty of the terrace, another shallow shelf in the mountain reached, curving, around the side. Aziz beckoned, and we followed. This "north terrace" is really more like a road, leading around the peak to the stunning size and sweep of the East Terrace, the heart of the sanctuary. Here, looming above central court on a raised podium, are the remains of five enthroned deities, tall as five-story buildings from the base of the podium to the top of their carved stone heads. All the heads have fallen down now, rattled by earthquakes or buffeted by storms. When Theresa Goell first saw Nemrud Dagh, one head still stood on its carved body: that of the goddess Fortuna, the only female among the enshrined deities and an ancient pagan goddess of fertility. She wears a veil and a turban of fruit, and Miss Goell proclaimed proudly as recently as 1961 that "the lady had kept her head." Now even the lady lies on the ground with the rest, the victim of a bolt of lightning in the mid-1960s. She, like the others, is much too heavy to be reinstalled, although workmen have carefully set her right side up again.

When they were new, the great gods sat with their backs to the mountaintop, their sightless eyes facing toward a sort of Persian fire altar and across it toward the east. The terrain falls away sharply down the side of Nemrud Dagh and across miles and miles of sere, jagged peaks and crags toward Syria, Iraq, Iran, India . . . I remembered, gazing out that way, that when I first met Theresa Goell I was struck by her expression of amazement. She looked amazed all the time, as if the expression had frozen on her face. Now, looking at her mountain, I understood.

Antiochus' pantheon was deliberately designed to merge, to fuse, the varying religions and myths of his crossroads kingdom. It is therefore one of the most revealing of the mystery cults in that last century before the rise of Christianity, when the pagan

gods of East and West met in Commagene. At the extreme left of
the line of five figures was a "fused" god identified as Apollo (a
name used by both Greeks and Romans); as Helios and Hermes,
the Greek gods of the sun and of roads, commerce, and invention; and also as Mithras, the Persian equivalent of Apollo. Next
to him was the goddess Fortuna; and in the place of honor in the
middle was the "Thunder Shaker," the Father of the Gods, Zeus
himself. Here Zeus was also identified as Ahura Mazda and as
Oromasdes, alternative names for the supreme deity of a Persian
religion founded in the sixth century B.C. by Zoroaster. At Zeus'
left hand sat King Antiochus with the headdress of a deity, and
at *his* left was a synthesized god of war and of strength, the Greek
Herakles—also identified with Ares and Mars, the Greek and
Roman gods of war, and with the character we know as Hercules
the strong.

Behind the seated figures, in the base of the podium, were
incised long inscriptions in Greek, and along the walls were
Greco-Persian portraits of Darius the Great and of a beautiful
woman who may have been Antiochus' wife or his mother. They
had been skillfully carved. Whose hands had done this work? Aziz
could only shrug his shoulders. I remembered a sentence Theresa
Goell had written in the *National Geographic* of March, 1961:
"The singular beauty of these portraits . . . establishes this sanctuary as one of the glories of the Hellenistic world, not—as had
formerly been thought—the crude product of a semi-barbarian
monarch."

Dominating even the great seated gods, however, was that
strange, perfectly cone-shaped, artificial mound, or tumulus,
which rose to a peak behind their heads. Perhaps the unknown
sculptors had built it just as a means for disposing of their surplus
rock as they carved it away. But Theresa Goell for years was convinced that it served another purpose entirely: she believed that
the tumulus covered the tomb of Antiochus I. If it could be
found, if it had never been looted, if it existed at all, it would
provide the world with a new and rare look at the customs, the
personal accouterments, and the treasure of a little-known king of
the first century before Christ.

Attempts to dig into the cone did nothing but set off small rock-

Kenan, our driver, rests beside Apollo.

Kenan the driver, at left, talks to Aziz, standing beside the head of Herakles.

Near the summit, the symmetrical peak of the tumulus of Nemrud Dagh rises against the sky. In the foreground, wearing a hat, is the Turkish archaeologist whom we named "the Commissar."

slides: all the rocks appeared to be fist-sized or slightly larger, and they simply rolled and shifted. Either the entire tumulus would have to be taken down and carried off the mountain, or the archaeologists would have to find a way to explore through the heap of stones to locate the burial chamber beneath. Miss Goell had read of the work of an Italian tomb-finder named Carlo M. Lerici, who used electrical and seismic soundings to locate cavities and archaeological remains deep under the earth, and in 1963 the National Geographic Society sponsored an expedition to Nemrud Dagh that included a team of Lerici technicians.

First they tried the seismic method. Light charges of dynamite were fired into the rubble, creating seismic waves. Then the technicians measured the time taken by the waves to cover a given distance. The speed of a sound wave depends upon ground density and the properties of various kinds of materials—bedrock or rubble or empty space—and it is usually a reliable method for finding a deeply buried hollow. The howling winds of Nemrud Dagh scrambled the sound waves so confusingly, however, that seismic testing had to be abandoned. Then the expedition tried the electrical-resistivity method. In this, charges of electrical current are sent into the ground and delicate instruments measure the amount of resistance these waves encounter. Empty space resists such charges far more strongly than does rock or rubble. Thus, the sudden flick of a measuring needle, indicating strong resistance, also indicates the presence of a cavity. It could of course be a natural cave in the rock, or it could be a tomb. The instruments did find one such cavity, on the East Terrace below and in front of the statue of the enthroned Zeus.

In 1964 Miss Goell went back, this time with a new crew of experts, and they attacked the tumulus and the terraces with everything science has thought up to date and even with a stone-cutting diamond drill. They dug into the "cavity" on the East Terrace—and found nothing except some red soil striation, which may actually have accounted for the magnetic signals they got the year before. The 1964 study did provide an accurate measurement of the depth and amount of loose tumulus and the size of the mountain's rock core. And it indicated that right at the top, hidden under the fist-sized boulders, is a sort of saddle or indentation. It could be the remains of an old roadway used by Antiochus' builders to haul their rubble up to the top, or it might even lead to a tunnel or passage which itself could lead to the long-lost tomb.

Still, the tomb was never found, and as the scientists struggled back down the mountain, carrying their sophisticated equipment, the words of Antiochus himself must have rung in their ears. In a Holy Edict in Greek which he left on the top of the mountain, the King said that his tomb "is to be indestructible by the ravages of time." And also, at this point, the ravages of diggers.

We were all reluctant to leave that arrogant but appealing king; to say farewell to his gods and his guardian lions and eagles, to the great windswept reaches of his old domain. It was most difficult of all perhaps because in that time-haunted place it was so easy to believe, with Antiochus, that this mountain was indeed "in closest proximity to the heavenly throne." Halfway, as Meezgole had said, between earth and heaven.

We started down the mountain at 2:30 in the afternoon. Was it the same day, or a week later?

Down was, in total defiance of the law of gravity and of all those stern moral preachments about the treacherous ease of the Downward Path, a great deal more difficult than up. Down was, in a word, awful. Mules stumble more often going down, for one thing, and for another thing it's so much easier to see, straight ahead, the jagged rock upon which your head will be crushed if you fall off. Before we reached Horuk again it had begun to sprinkle, and the Nemrud Dagh red dust with which we had become impregnated turned to mud on sunglasses, on clothes, even on the mule. The storm darkened the sky, and in a flash I remembered both that beastly rocky river and the steep stone bridge, and I remembered Theresa Goell's account of a carved stele, or stone slab, King Antiochus had left way down in the valley below his sanctuary. The stele warned those who approached unwarily, or with lack of respect, or with intention to desecrate the holy place, either to flee instantly or to suffer the consequences. Quickly I offered a silent prayer to all the gods—all of Antiochus' and all of mine—and a quick *Mashallah* for good measure, and hoped that my awe at the top would compensate for that one moment of heady abandon when I had gaily tossed a roll of color film from somewhere around the shoulders of Zeus down to my friend standing beside the head of Fortuna. "No offense, Your Majesties," I muttered, clutching the rear of the saddle with both hands.

The sun set before we reached the stream, and an explosion of color backlighted the crags and the twisted trees. Stars came out, and once we caught the faint glimmer of kerosene lamps in Eski Kahta, but they looked ten miles away. Kenan had stopped shouting *Yahooo!* and the drivers had stopped shouting *Kootch!*

and the hour had turned suddenly to grim endurance. Rigor mortis had affected all my limbs and was creeping toward the head: I couldn't decide whether I was frightened of the dark or glad that I couldn't see where the mule was going. The leader, who had walked and walked this long day, was now leaping from side to side in the dark, feeling his way with a sense as sure as the mule's, and lifting a strong arm out of the blackness now and then to steady me when he knew, and the mule knew, that we were going to make a sudden lurch in some unforeseen direction. My friend called out of the black, "How much longer do you think it will be?" and I heard the fatigue in her voice. I thought half an hour, but I said an hour, just in case. Then I began to prepare mentally for the crucial maneuver of getting off the mule. I would not fall off; I would not collapse in a heap. That tall mule . . . it had looked so safe, that morning, and now it seemed so impossibly high.

As it turned out, nobody fell off. We must all have ridden that last hour with a growing desire to dismount with dignity, as befitted the King. I slid, slowly, to the ground on trembling legs, and the leader held out his hand silently. I shook it, and I fought an overpowering desire to kiss him and to kiss the mule. I would have, had they not both been Turkish and averse to such unseemly extravagances on the part of foreign women.

There was some discussion of driving back to Adiyaman that night, but nobody could face it. The heroic Aziz, who had once been headman of the village, offered his home for the night, and everybody accepted. His living room was very like that of the Nemrud Dagh guard: a beaten-earth floor covered with carpets, kerosene lamps suspended from wall brackets, two shelves at the far ends of the room. We staggered inside, and those who could still bend either sat down or lay down. The mule leaders came inside and, apparently unaffected by ten hours of steady walking up and down, removed their shoes and squatted on the floor with their knees touching their ears. I thought my own leader deserved a bonus because of his particularly tall, strong mule, and my companion thought her leader deserved a bonus because he had risked life and limb on the descent to dart down a precipice and pick for her a beautiful golden flower.

No bonuses were forthcoming, however, from Aziz, who considers the journey routine, so while the wages were paid and we all attempted to resume breathing, I passed around two or three more sacks of nuts. There was very little conversation. Oral the interpreter was flat out on one shelf, breathing heavily; my brown-eyed friend had apparently expired on the opposite shelf; Kenan and the Commissar were on the floor groaning in duet and massaging their aching legs. Aziz and I were still upright— he because he wasn't tired and I because I didn't dare bend anywhere for fear of breakage.

Then an astonishing thing happened: the mule drivers vanished—just vanished, without a farewell and without my even noticing their departure. They must have stood one by one and slipped silently out the door. When they were gone I looked around the room, and there sat a man I had never seen before in my life. He hadn't said a word; he was just sitting there, with his knees beside his ears, and he looked like all mule leaders except that he wasn't one. Who he was, and when he had joined our group, I never discovered. He was still sitting there, silent, immobile, when Aziz came in carrying a huge brass tray on carved wooden legs. He put it in the center of the room, disappeared again, and came back with a pilaf of cracked wheat, a delicious green salad, white cheese, eggs, and heaps of flat bread. It was agony to move a leg or an arm to reach the dinner, but we all managed it.

Then Aziz banished the men, explaining that the living room, with its two shelves, was the ladies' bedroom. He had commandeered enormous, thick comforters from all the village, and he spread them grandly on the two shelves for our beds. He lighted the kerosene lamps, opened an escape window for the fumes, and staggered in with pillows. For some reason, the Turks in this region use pillows that seem to be made of lead; they weigh about a ton each and are so stubbornly resistant that even after six hours the head can't make a dent in them. For anyone who needs his head propped up, however, there is nothing better.

Aziz then turned to me and said, quite clearly, "Wash wash."

"Wash wash?" I replied. Not a very clever answer, but I was tired.

"Wash wash," he said firmly.

Okay, I'm dirty, I thought. If this grand man, who took us up the mountain and back, wants me to wash, then certainly I will wash. Meekly I followed him out of the room, across the hall, and into a cubicle in which were an enormous barrel of water, a footstool, and a hole in the floor. Aziz motioned that I should take off my shoes and socks, and he would wash my feet.

I was appalled. Someone else should wash my feet? Someone as grand as Aziz? Never. I was saved by a technicality: I was wearing a body stocking under my slacks, and by sign language I conveyed to Aziz that to take off my socks I would have to strip from the waist down. It was his turn to be appalled. He fled, and I assured him that I would "wash wash" by myself. Then I cheated. To have taken off everything and then to have drenched my aching limbs in cold water would have been tantamount to suicide. At least, so I thought. I picked up a sponge and a bucket and I threw water all around the room, but never on myself. The water made a gurgling noise, and I thought craftily that it would have fooled even my mother. After a suitable interval, I emerged, and I made happy clean gestures in the air. "Nothing like a bath," I said loudly.

Aziz came back one more time, quietly, to make sure each of us was safely installed on a shelf. Then, gently, he lifted the comforters one by one and placed them over us.

"Nemrud Dagh Hotel," he said, laughing.

It was 8:45 P.M. It was the hardest bed I had ever slept upon. The air was thick with kerosene, and every time I shut my eyes I felt that mule again, going *down*. I clutched the side of the bed and mourned for my destroyed muscles, but I couldn't sleep. Aziz was outside, talking, talking, talking. Obviously there were problems in the village, and he was the former headman. Eventually I dozed, and I felt the mule and I heard Aziz and I saw Meezgole, and in my dreams I had become a latter-day Antiochus and I was sitting on the peak, that incredible peak, ordering a statue to be erected forthwith to the man Aziz. I was wondering how precisely to render his mustache when—again—it was 4:30 A.M. and time to get into the red Ford and start back.

There is a postscript to this story. We all arose at 4:30, and we drove back through Kahta to Adiyaman, and almost all the way we could see the little blue peak of Nemrud Dagh. The sun came up behind it and turned it flaming red, and at that moment I couldn't believe that I had been there—had stood on it. The men were silent, and they too kept looking at the mountain.

When we got to Adiyaman, about 8 o'clock in the morning, we bumped into Meezgole in the square. She pretended that her business with the governor had kept her over another day. Perhaps. I believe that she stayed over just to see the eyes of those who had just looked at Nemrud Dagh, and to read in those eyes the wonder she has never lost.

We sat down over tea and olives and cheese and we all babbled at once, and then the Turkish archaeologist tapped his spoon on his glass and said to Miss Goell, quite clearly, quite specifically, and in English, "Thank you. Thank you for Nemrud Dagh."

When the archaeologist gives back to the world a lost and forgotten kingdom, a moment of glory, he gives it to all men. But the Commissar knew that the glory is restored most intimately perhaps to the nation in which it lies. He, as a Turk and an archaeologist, was grateful, and he was gracious. His short speech was worthy of the mountain, of himself, of Aziz, and of Meezgole.

4

OLDER THAN HISTORY

History is to most of us, in the simplest terms, all the things that happened before we arrived on the scene. Occasionally there seems to be too much of it, but at least the parts we are required to learn are written down and can be taken in large or small doses.

This is not true of much of the country we call Turkey. Great cities and cultures lived and died there at the dawn of writing or even before it, and thus were deprived of their own "history" for the lack of a comprehensible written record. In recent times scholars have tended to lump these early sites together in the simple geographical reference "Anatolia," meaning the great central plain of the peninsula of Turkey.

Archaeology is writing Turkey's complete, true history—writing it the hard way by prying out of the debris and silence of millennia the remains of those great dead civilizations.

"I am a professor of history; that is my training and my career," a Turkish Education Minister named Hikmet Gurçay once told me; "but I did not know about my own country many of the things I am learning every month from the archaeologists. It is they who are discovering our history, and they who are writing it.

The new history books in Turkey and in all the world will be better because of them."

To the scholars of the classical world, the Greece and Rome we know so much about, "history" effectively began about 1194 B.C., the date given for the beginning of the Trojan War. Ancient scholars learned about the war from the epic account the *Iliad*, ascribed to the poet Homer, although some considered it a work of fiction and some even doubted that a man named Homer ever existed. Before Homer wrote Trojan history for those long-ago scholars, of course, there were already folk tales in existence, tales about the creation of the earth and of men. These stories were a kind of prehistory in themselves, though they were originally told, not written, and they existed more as a part of primitive religions than of historical fact.

Both the Tigris and the Euphrates, the great rivers that provided the cradle for Western man, rise in eastern Turkey and flow through it for miles and miles before they meet near the Persian Gulf on the border of modern Iraq and Iran. Near them once lived an Anatolian people who sheltered in caves and left primitive drawings incised in the rock. Later, but still almost nine thousand years ago, human beings on the Anatolian plain began one of their first experiments in living together, in permanent cities. The first cities were characterized by great mutual-defense walls, and by the presence of individuals who didn't spend all their days hunting for food but instead had time to paint paintings and make decorative objects to sell. Archaeologists discovered, in the late 1950s, just such a one of these first cities, called Çatal Hüyük, in a typical mound formation. Excavation is far from complete, but there were at least twelve levels of habitation at Çatal Hüyük, and the people who lived there had to get into their houses from the roof, on a ladder, because there were no doors and few windows.

About 3000 B.C., writing was invented, but by then several great cultures of the Anatolian plain had gone into decline or disappeared, and of those who came after, so few persons wrote that they were all but forgotten. A still little-known agricultural group called the Hatti lived there, and they were pushed aside by a great wave of migrants called the Hittites. Behind the Hittites came the Phrygians, whose greatest king was Midas, he of the golden touch. Phrygian domination was brief, but it left the world a kind of conical, soft headgear known as the Phrygian cap which is still worn by the female personification of France, Marianne, who is to Frenchmen what Uncle Sam is to Americans. We may still admire the Phrygian cap on French coins, postage stamps, and patriotic posters featuring Marianne. We may also admire a version of it in the triple-tiered crown worn by Popes in Rome; the tiered crown is a descendant of the Phrygian cap. The Phrygians, in turn, were overrun by invaders called Cimmerians —who may have been nomadic, as their record is brief in Anatolia and has left us mainly the name Crimea to celebrate its passing.

Just as Antiochus' little kingdom of Commagene was a crossroads of the world in the south, the whole Anatolian peninsula was a highway for a bewildering succession of migrant tribes and would-be conquerors. They met here, collided, caromed off each other like billard balls. It is all too complex to remember clearly. About 400 B.C., ten thousand Greek mercenary soldiers were left stranded by the death of their leader, Cyrus, in Babylonia, but even though leaderless, they managed to march across the Anatolian plain all the way to the sea at a town called Trabzon. Their feat was celebrated by an Athenian patriot and writer, Xenophon. Alexander the Great stormed across Anatolia and nearly caught his death of cold from swimming in the chilly Cydnus River (now called the Tarsus River) in 333 B.C. Hannibal, being chased by Roman soldiers, ended up in Anatolia, and from about A.D. 1096 to 1100, thousands of Crusaders—some civilians and some the famous Knights of the Cross of the First Crusade—streamed across Anatolia headed for Jerusalem to rescue it from the faith and the soldiers of Islam. Genghis Khan, the fierce Mongolian warrior, crossed the plain in the thirteenth century on his conquering foray across most of the Near East and into Europe.

The Greeks established a string of colonies all along the western coastline, and then the Romans followed and conquered the Greeks. In the meantime, a great culture called Urartu grew up around Lake Van in the east, a culture unknown until archaeologists began digging there after World War II. Then there was Lycia, on the southern shore, Lycia with its haunting carved rock tombs, its famed archers, the nation for which all the "Lyceums" of the world (either buildings, or associations for public instruction by lectures) are named. And Caria, and Lydia, the kingdom ruled by King Croesus. The historian Herodotus (roughly 450 B.C.) said that the mysterious Etruscans who flourished in the center of Italy and left there magnificent painted tombs were actually Lydians who fled to Italy during a food shortage in their homeland. Archaeological evidence is now beginning to confirm that old story.

In eastern Anatolia lived the Armenians. This very much put-upon people, part of whose territory is now in the Soviet Union, were overrun throughout history by Persians, Arabs, Greeks, Romans, Egyptians, and in the end by the modern Turks themselves. The ultimate Armenian struggle against the Turks was the subject of a melodramatic classic called *The Forty Days of Musa Dagh*, by Franz Werfel, and resulted in an exhortation commonly used forty years ago by mothers whose children stubbornly refused to eat their supper. "Remember," they would say sternly; "remember the starving Armenians." I, personally, ate for them for years, remaining always skeptical about just how much good my eating was doing *them*.

Proud Turkey/Anatolia has never quite received the credit it deserves as a cradle of our mutual history because so many of its heroic figures were long thought to be just "legends" or because they were associated with Greece and Rome. People forget that the Greeks and Romans were for centuries all over the western and southern shores of Anatolia. Troy itself, with all the rolling Greek names—Helen, Paris, Hector, Menelaus, Ulysses, Achilles —is not in Greece; it is in Turkey.

Antony met Cleopatra not in Rome or in Egypt but in Turkey, in Saul's town of Tarsus, on the southern coast. There, the story goes, the townsfolk left Antony "enthroned in the market place" to rush down and greet Cleopatra arriving by sea. Tarsus isn't in fact on the sea, and if Cleopatra had to do it today she would never make it. But in those days there was a big lake into which the river Cydnus ran, and it was connected by a canal to the Mediterranean. The lake has since silted full, and even the Cydnus River itself has some difficulty getting to the sea.

The poet Homer was born in Turkey, as were the Greek historians Herodotus and Strabo. Even Santa Claus had his beginnings in Turkey, as St. Nicholas. There is still in the Antalya museum, in Turkey, a casket that is supposed to contain his bones. But there is also in Bari, Italy, an immense and ancient church called San Nicola which was founded in 1087 specifically to house the "relics" of the saint. Poor St. Nicholas: like many another popular saint, he has enough "genuine" bones attributed to him to make quite a respectable dinosaur.

His actual life is almost as hazy as his fame is enormous. Probably he was born in Patara, around A.D. 300. Later he rose in the early Christian church to become Bishop of Myra, in what is now southeastern Turkey. Some say he was persecuted for his faith and was killed about A.D. 345; at least, his name appears in some ninth-century lists of Christian martyrs. Certainly there was a shrine to his memory in the eleventh century, and the faithful went there to worship his remains and other holy objects. All was fairly orderly until the year 1087, when some larcenous sailors from Bari, Italy, decided they would steal the St. Nicholas relics, Those were days in which pirates and brigands roamed the Mediterranean, and things on shore were little better as the local potentates fought for power. When the Bari sailors got to Myra they found that the town had just been conquered by a nearby caliph, and St. Nicholas' shrine had been abandoned by all except a handful of monks. Somehow the sailors persuaded the monks that they had authority to take away the relics. They took, the story says, an urn half filled with oil, a heap of jumbled bones, and a skull which was separated from the rest of the skeleton. Once they got back to Bari, they distributed dollops of the "holy oil" to monasteries and churches, and bits of bone to other sacred institutions. A French bishop crossed the Alps in 1100 just to get a phial of the oil from St. Nicholas' tomb.

At about the same time as the "Bari raid," some other sailors from Venice went off to Myra to steal the relics too. They got there too late, but when they returned to Venice they too had

A marble carving, one of the few that show Santa Claus during his St. Nicholas period in Turkey, stands in the garden of the Archaeological Museum in Bodrum, the former Halicarnassus, on the southwestern shore.

some bones, which they proclaimed to be those of the *uncle* of St. Nicholas.

The worldwide fame of the saint seems to have originated in Bari, where every year even to this day a pilgrimage and a procession take place on his feast day. How he came to be associated with gifts and with Christmas is more of a mystery. One version says that he generously and quietly provided dowries for the three daughters of an impoverished citizen of Myra, and thus originated the practice of giving gifts in secret on the Eve of St. Nicholas, which is December 6. Slowly, through the years, he became more and more popular. He became the patron saint of old Russia, of Greece, of the Kingdom of Naples—and of mariners (because it was they who stole his relics, perhaps?), merchants, and children. The Dutch called him Sint Nicolaas, or Sinter Klaas, and took him with them to colonial America, where he became Santa Claus.

Many of the Hebrew heroes and Christian saints, the places and events of the Bible are rooted in what is now Turkey. In A.D. 330 the Roman Emperor Constantine moved his capital, and with it the weight of the Holy Roman Empire, from Rome to Anatolia and named the new capital—today's Istanbul—Constantinople. This was the Byzantine Empire, and it lasted for 1,000 years. When it fell, to the Ottoman Turks, Christianity fell with it on the Anatolian peninsula. The Turks brought with them the Islamic religion, and the inhabitants of Anatolia, fed up with the excesses of the Crusaders and the oppression of the Byzantine rulers, happily embraced Allah. Modern Turkey is 98 per cent Moslem.

But for a hair's breadth, so would be much of Eastern Europe today, for the Turks were such fierce fighters and superb horsemen that they overran not only the Anatolian peninsula but also Greece, North Africa, and the territory that is modern Yugoslavia, Hungary, Rumania. They were halted at last in an epic battle called the siege of Vienna, just east of that Austrian city, in 1683.

The Turkey we know today—still Eastern in many of its traditions and customs, but Western and European by choice and direction—is the creation of an astonishing twentieth-century strong-man/reformer, Mustafa Kemal Ataturk. He was born in 1881 and, like all Turks of that era, was given only one name, Mustafa. It is Moslem practice to give one name and then, for clarity, add a descriptive word to it. The name "Kemal," which means "perfection," was given him by a schoolmaster who was obviously impressed by him. The name "Ataturk," which means "Father Turk," was the final addition when he became the father of the new Turkey. A career army officer whose travels convinced him that the Western nations were more progressive than the Eastern ones, he became his country's popular hero after World War I. At that moment the victorious Allies showed every sign of intending to carve up Turkey and parcel it out among themselves. Ataturk rallied the army and the peasants and drove the Allies off Turkish territory. Then in rapid succession he deposed the reigning Sultan, got rid of the Caliph who was supreme religious leader of the nation, and launched his stunned countrymen onto a breakneck charge into the 20th century. He reformed both the language and the alphabet, getting rid of Arabic words and altering Turkish into a Latinized language. This can lead to some wonderfully amusing words in modern Turkish, many taken over from the French or Italian or English and spelled phonetically for ease in learning: *vagon-restoran* for dining car, *otel* for hotel, *banyo* for bathroom, *tost-sandoviç* for a toasted sandwich. It is a boon for the foreigner who doesn't speak Turkish, too: the oddest-looking word, if pronounced phonetically, will suddenly be comprehensible.

Ataturk also abolished the fez for men—a conical red felt cap usually with a black tassel, which he considered too "Eastern"—and the veil for women. He moved the capital of the nation from ancient Constantinople to the straggling interior village of Ankara, and set about building schools and emancipating women. It was all too fast for many a proud and conservative Turkish peasant, but by the time Ataturk died in 1938 his nation was allied with Europe in trade and in military treaties.

Just as modern Turkey has taken over words from the West, so the West has for years taken words and expressions from Anatolia and the richness of the land that is older than history. The "whirl-

FİAT LİSTESİ		
CİNSİ	LİRA	Krs.
ÇAY	1	00
ÇİÇEK	1	00
KAHVE	1	50
GAZOZ - AYRAN	1	00
PEPSİKOLA - FRUKO	1	50
SUNALKO	1	50
COCA COLA	1	50
BİRA	2	50
DEMLİK ÇAY (İKİLİ)	2	50
MADEN SUYU	1	00
MENBA		25
TOST - SANDOVİÇ	1	00
NARGİLE	2	50
UMUMİ GİRİŞ		50
HAVUZLAR SAHASINA GİRİŞ	1	00
YÜZME ÜCRETİ (2. SAAT)	2	50
KABİN	1	00
MASA	2	50
MAYO	1	00
ÖZEL AİLE BANYOLARI (1. SAAT)	10	00

AYRICA GARSONİYE YOKTUR
ŞİKAYETLERİNİZİ İDAREYE BİLDİRİNİZ.

A tourist menu near Denizli shows the odd phonetic spelling of modern Turkish. Çay, at the top, means tea; kahve is coffee; tost-sandoviç means a toasted sandwich.

ing dervish" is Anatolian—an inheritance from a religious sect of the thirteenth century whose members achieved religious ecstasy through music and their whirling, swooping, graceful dances. Our word "assassin" derives from Turkish, coming from a corruption of "hashish." This drug was used in ancient Anatolia to turn men into bloodthirsty warriors. "Meander" comes from the name of an Anatolian river that couldn't make up its mind whether to head for the Mediterranean or for the Black Sea. "Mausoleum" comes from a King of Caria, in Anatolia, called Mausolus. When he died his widow erected the famous tomb at Halicarnassus, one of the seven wonders of the ancient world, and the king's name, in the word "mausoleum," lasted longer than the tomb.

It is one of the great triumphs of the archaeologists that they have made the wonderful old legends come true: there *was* a Troy and a Trojan war; there *were* a rich King Croesus and Midas and a "Gordian knot," whether or not Alexander the Great ever actually severed it, as tradition has it. But even more exciting, archaeologists don't stop here. They go back, back, before the Greeks and the Romans, back into the mists before the legends and before written history. Anatolians probably invented coinage and wine making; they may well have been the first to discover ironworking. Even before that—eight, nine, ten thousand years ago—they crept out of the caves and the forests and created a town, a proper town (it may have been a bad idea, but it represented progress at the time) in which they raised houses and temples, painted pictures celebrating a cult of bull worship, and made little clay figurines to the glory of a mother/fertility figure.

"Turkey is the most important archaeological site in the world today," said proud Education Minister Gurçay. "Because it goes through all the centuries of civilized man. No other nation has it all."

5

THE GREAT CODE-BREAKERS

A bearded, eccentric Swiss who called himself "Sheik Ibrahim," a couple of wandering American tourists, an Irish missionary and a short-tempered Egyptian peasant woman who threw rocks at some trespassing foreigners provided the clues for one of the most exciting archaeological discoveries in the world—the great empire of the Hittites.

The Hittites, a still somewhat enigmatic people who moved into Anatolia about four thousand years ago, absorbed some of the language and culture of the tribes they found already there, and then proceeded to annex territory and peoples on all sides until they became a nation as powerful as neighboring Babylonia or even mighty Egypt under the Pharaohs, far away to the south. Then, about 1180 B.C., the main Hittite cities fell in what must have been such a sudden, catastrophic military defeat that even the Hittite traditions all but vanished from the minds of men.

A few echoes of them did turn up in the Bible: in the book of Genesis, for example, Abraham asks "the sons of Heth" (now identified as Hittites) for permission to buy in their land a burial place for his wife Sarah. Elsewhere it is noted that King David coveted the wife of "Uriah the Hittite." But most Biblical references lumped the Hittites in with a number of small tribes in and around the general region of today's Syria, in the sort of "census reference" which most Bible readers leap over as quickly as they do that long, tiresome list of the "begats." One of those typical census-taking references occurs in Numbers, 13:29: "The Amalekites dwell in the land of the Negeb; the Hittites, the Jebusites, and the Amorites dwell in the hill country, and the Canaanites dwell by the sea, and along the Jordan."

Just a hundred years ago German scholars, who are not known for their reticence in matters scientific and scholarly, brushed off the once-mighty Hittites with only seven lines in Germany's most authoritative encyclopedia, calling them a "Canaanite tribe encountered by the Israelites in Palestine." Actually, almost all the important clues to the real power of the Hittites had been found by that time, but the archaeological detectives had not yet put them together. The Hittites referred to in the Bible were the remnants of the once-great empire, later and less important Hittites who lived far south of the former seat of their big cities.

The first man to note and record one of the vital clues was a fellow as exotic and mysterious as the Hittites themselves, "Sheik Ibrahim." In 1809 he set out from the island of Malta, just south of Sicily in the Mediterranean, headed for Syria. He said he was a merchant and that he worked for the British East India Company. Once in Syria, however, he did very little trading. Instead, he steeped himself in local culture. He studied the Koran, the Bible of the Moslems, and he set himself to learning the languages and customs of the Middle East. Every now and again he went off on a long trip; he was once arrested in Nubia, the land just below Egypt, as a spy and was hustled out of the country. Once he so impressed two Arabian scholars with his brilliant knowledge of Moslem law and custom that he was granted permission to go to the "forbidden city," the holy Mecca, and permitted to stay there for an unprecedented four months. This entitled him forever to the title of "Haji," meaning a man who has been to the holy city. He died very young, at thirty-three, in Cairo, and he was buried there as a "Haji."

Just why this man wanted to be a "sheik" we probably will never know for sure. His real name was Johann Ludwig Burckhardt, and he was born into a wealthy and aristocratic family in Basel, Switzerland, in 1784. Probably his motivation was a search for knowledge: he wanted to find out what was *there*—the same as Christopher Columbus did; or Lewis and Clark; or Sir Edmund Hillary, the conqueror of Mt. Everest; or the astronauts in our era.

On one of his journeys, Sheik Ibrahim/Johann Burckhardt passed through the city of Hama in Syria, the Hamath of the Bible. There, embedded in one wall of a building in the bazaar, he saw a stone covered with small signs and symbols. It appeared to him to be some form of hieroglyphic writing, but it was totally different from that of the Egyptians, the most familiar hieroglyphs of the Middle East. He noted it briefly in his travel journal and went on his way. Not until five years after his death, in 1822, was this first mention of the now-famous "Hamath stone" made public in travel journals and diaries published by the Royal Geographical Society in London. No one paid any attention at all. Had Sheik Ibrahim lived a little longer and had time to look at that stone again, or had he stopped to make a sketch of its strange symbols, the world might have discovered the Hittites a century before it did.

Sixty years later, the Hamath stone was "discovered" again, this time by an American Consul General, Augustus Johnson. He was having a day's outing with a missionary friend named Dr. Jessup, and they went, as all tourists will, to the bazaar. There they spotted that strangely carved stone, and they talked about it. The natives assured them that it was nothing unusual. There were three more just like it, they said, in the neighborhood. Johnson and Dr. Jessup wanted to copy the mysterious hieroglyphs on the stone, but the Syrians instantly distrusted the "infidels." This is the same word, by the way, that the Christian Crusaders had hurled as an epithet against the Moslems in Jerusalem only a few centuries earlier; it means nothing more ominous than "nonbeliever." In any case, the Syrians in the crowd in the Hama bazaar that day became so fierce that the Americans made a tactical retreat both from the strange stone and from the bazaar itself.

In the next few years at least two other groups of Westerners

One of the "Hamath stones," long embedded in a village wall, now in the Archaeological Museum in Istanbul. The inscription says: "Irtames, King of Hamath, son of Urhilina, erected the ramparts of his city. During this construction some cities helped Hamath by sending stones for the construction."

tried to have a good look at the stone, and each time the villagers of Hama drove them away. Finally, annoyed by this constant intrusion, they threatened to destroy the stone completely. Intervention came in the person of Subhi Pasha, the Turkish governor of Syria. At this point, in 1872, the Ottoman Turkish Empire ruled much of the world around it, and Syria was a province of Turkey. Subhi Pasha was a man of education and intellectual curiosity, and he decided to go and have a look at this stone that was causing such an uproar in the bazaar. He took with him the British Consul from Damascus and an Irish missionary named William Wright, who was an accomplished linguist and Biblical scholar. He also took along, just to be sure, a detachment of armed troops. That turned out to have been a good idea.

This group of explorers quickly found the stone, and were shown the three others. One was stuck in a garden wall, one in a house, another in a small shop. Sometime during the centuries, they had been picked up by the villagers and used simply as structural stone. All but one of them, that is: one, the villagers swore, was a miraculous curer of rheumatic pains. Sufferers would come to touch it or lie on it, and then pray like fury to both Mohammed and the Christian saints. When the Reverend Mr. Wright wanted to remove the stones, so that scholars could study their strange symbols, the natives objected.

Subhi Pasha, beckoning his troops forward, offered politely to pay for the stones so that the villagers could buy others to replace them in the house, and the bazaar wall, and the garden. Reluctantly, the villagers fell back, and the troops removed the stones and carried them to the Pasha's guesthouse. That night the villagers came back, however, and shouted loudly outside the guesthouse for the return of their stones. Even more exciting than this near-riot was a spectacular shower of meteors which lighted the sky and terrified the populace. That night the villagers fled, but the next morning they were back, and they said that the "rain of stars" had been a sign from the gods that the stones should not be removed from Hama.

First, to calm them, Subhi Pasha handed over the money he had promised to pay. Then he seems to have conducted himself like a latter-day Solomon. Had the "rain of stars" actually fallen on anyone and hurt him, he asked? The villagers admitted that nobody had been hurt. Then had the rain of stars possibly killed an ox, or a sheep, or damaged a house? No, again. Well then, said the Pasha reasonably, could not the great meteor display have been a sign of Heaven's consent? Could it not even be a celebration that the wonderful stones had been found and would be sent away to tell their secrets to the larger world? After all, the fireworks had been impressive, and no damage had been done.

Whether it was the Pasha's logic that prevailed or the Pasha's soldiers may remain forever moot. But the stones were taken away in November, 1872, and sent to the capital of the Ottoman Empire, Constantinople, to be displayed and studied in a national museum. The Pasha permitted the indefatigable William Wright to make casts of them to be sent to the British Museum in London.

Almost at the same time, a stone covered with the same incomprehensible hieroglyphics turned up in Aleppo, also in Syria, and here, as in Hama, the stone was considered to hold magic power. Its surface had been worn almost smooth by the foreheads, cheeks, and eyelashes of simple people afflicted with ophthalmia, an eye inflammation common in the Middle East. For centuries the peasants had believed that if they rubbed their aching eyes on this stone, they would be cured; it takes a lot of cheeks, a lot of eyelashes, to wear away the carving on a basalt block.

Why this fixation with the healing powers of strange stones nobody could read? The urge to touch a monument (or to scribble on it) seems to be universal, but these stones were not monuments—at least not to the persons who lay on them, or rubbed their eyes on them. It is tempting to believe that some deep, unrecognized but potent folk memory impelled the people to "worship" these stones: they touched them and prayed for a miracle, a gesture that is very close to worship. Here in this corner of the world where great religions grew—Judaism, Christianity, Islam—there must have been a constant blurring of lines and an exchange of ideas, a constant transmission through the centuries of history that lies beyond history, of events larger than men but universal among men. Something about the very mystery of the stones leaped across the millennia and spoke to the simple, superstitious descendants of all those fighting, worshiping vanished nations.

Quite another type of tale is that of the cache of written clues which turned up about five years later and 600 miles away, in Egypt. Modern airliners make such a trip in an hour and minutes, but in the 1880s it was a journey of many days, and four thousand years ago it was a world away—the southern limit of civilization.

Nevertheless, there in Egypt, at a place called Tell el-Amarna along the banks of the Nile, about 225 miles upriver from Cairo (it looks down, on a map, but the Nile flows from mid-Africa north toward the Mediterranean. So down is up, and backward on the map into Africa is "upriver" on the Nile), an Egyptian peasant woman was out one day gathering what Egyptians call *sebakh*. *Sebakh* is nothing but the crumbled old mud brick left behind from vanished houses and cities, the stuff of mounds. Egyptians had found that it made excellent fertilizer. As she trudged about picking up this ready-made and handy-sized soil fertilizer, the woman happened upon a pile of baked-clay tablets. They were the same color and basic material as the simple brick of houses, and the woman cared not a whit that they had some kind of writing on them. It is most unlikely that she could read writing of any kind anyway, so she was not impressed by her find.

At this exact point in the story, versions vary as to what happened next. Some sources say that she put the tablets into a sack and gave them to somebody to carry off to the nearest village. Other sources say that she was surprised at her work by a party of foreign travelers, and that she was so startled and offended by their presence that she threw some of the tablets at them to drive them off. I personally tend to believe that this version is true. How can one keep sheep, dogs, strays, and picnickers out of the garden except by throwing things at them? The woman thwarted herself. Because the strangers, who retreated under the barrage, noted the writing on the tablets, and as soon as the woman went away, they rushed back with new enthusiasm to find more.

This unnamed peasant woman had happened, by blind accident, upon the site of the long-deserted capital of the Pharaoh

Iknaton (circa 1350 B.C.), an idealistic and heretical leader who may have been the first ruler in all recorded history to declare that there was only one God instead of a lot of "gods." He broke away from the customs of earlier Egypt and set up a new capital at Tell el-Amarna. He also promptly had trouble both with his own people and with the neighbors. The Tell el-Amarna tablets, found in 1887, included a great number of copies of letters, written on clay and dispatched by courier, to the Pharaoh's allies in Syria and Palestine asking them to help him defend his dominion from some great power in the north whom he called the "Kheta" people. There were also two letters written in a totally unknown language which seemed to refer to something or someone called "Arzawa," whoever or whatever that might have been. Ironically, the tablets from the Pharaoh's great library of state were considered fakes by many people who saw them, and a great many tablets were destroyed before the scholars realized what they had in their hands.

By devious means the stones of Hamath and Aleppo, and the clay tablets of Tell el-Amarna, found their way to museums, and there the great code-breakers of the nineteenth century set to work on them. They were a strange breed, those men who, a hundred years ago, deciphered many of the ancient hieroglyphics. A great many of them were clergymen who had learned to read the ancient languages of the Middle East—Greek, Hebrew, Babylonian, Akkadian, Egyptian—out of simple desire to know the Bible better, to understand its historical references more clearly. They were also, of course, explorers of the mind, men who plunged with infinite patience into a maze of dusty fragments searching for uncharted lands the way Sheik Ibrahim had searched on foot.

The first man who ever suggested in print that possibly the mysterious stones were written by "Hittites" was the missionary William Wright. He said the writing must be that of the "sons of Heth," and he daringly added that these people had once been rulers of Syria and allies of mighty Egypt. This latter conclusion was extremely perceptive of the Reverend Mr. Wright, because he took it straight from the Bible. Ignoring the minor "census" references which had already been noted, he found a reference in the Second Book of Kings, 7:6, which said: "For the Lord had made the host of the Syrians to hear a noise of chariots . . . and they said to one another, Lo, the king of Israel hast hired against us the kings of the Hittites, and the kings of the Egyptians . . ." Any good military strategist would suspect from this passage that the strength of the Hittites was similar to that of the Egyptians. How William Wright happened to put the proper emphasis on this passage is not known, but perhaps being an Irish missionary in Syria in the nineteenth century required a talent for military strategy as well as religion.

Wright's reputation was such that people paid attention to his theory. Yet how could "Hittites" strong enough to be allies of Egypt exist this way in Second Kings and be tossed off so casually in other books of the Bible, lumped in with minor tribes? Who on earth had they been, truly, and where did they live?

As the scholars applied themselves to the puzzle, they began to think, tentatively, that maybe there had been two different groups of Hittites, or if not that, then perhaps two different periods in history. Perhaps they began as small, scattered tribes and became powerful later. If that was true, it was odd that the Biblical writers didn't explain it. But what if they had been powerful first, before the Bible was written, and then had fallen? That would explain references to them as a smallish and unimportant tribe.

While they grappled with this question, the code-breakers came upon the second horn of the Hittite dilemma: there were two totally different sets of "Hittite" writing. One was cuneiform, the other hieroglyphic.

Cuneiform was native to the eastern languages of Persia and Assyria, and consisted in its simplest form of wedge-shaped symbols arranged in patterns to make letters or syllables of words.

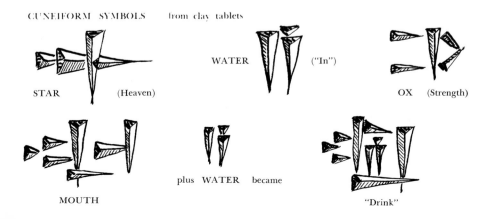

CUNEIFORM SYMBOLS   from clay tablets

STAR   (Heaven)

WATER   ("In")

OX   (Strength)

MOUTH

plus WATER   became

"Drink"

Hieroglyphic writing, on the other hand, is rooted in Egypt and is a series of pictograms, of tiny pictures which stand for recognizable objects, animals, situations, gestures and express not only finite objects but also actions.

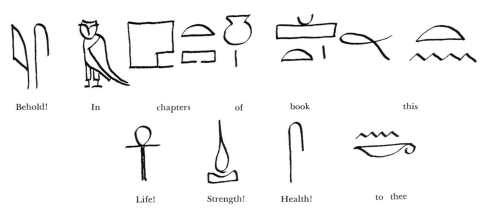

Behold!   In   chapters   of   book   this

Life!   Strength!   Health!   to thee

(Again, to comprehend in a nonscholarly way, consider the modern hieroglyph that playful U.S. and British soldiers invented in World War II just to tell anyone who passed by that they had been there. This was a simple line drawing of an elongated nose and a pair of hands, peering over a wall, a door, a trench, an upended tank. Sometimes these modern hieroglyphic writers appended an explanation, "Kilroy was here," but after a few months the explanation was no longer needed. Everybody knew what the hieroglyph meant.)

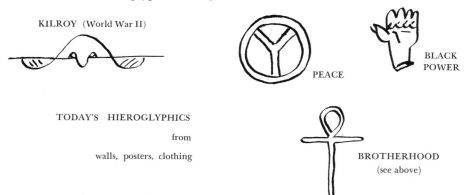

KILROY (World War II)

PEACE

BLACK POWER

TODAY'S HIEROGLYPHICS

from

walls, posters, clothing

BROTHERHOOD
(see above)

Linguistic scholars in the late nineteenth century could read both cuneiform and hieroglyphic, in that they knew what the symbols stood for, but that doesn't necessarily mean they could read the language. One can know the letters of the Roman alphabet, for example, but not be able to read them when they are put together in an unknown language.

Nevertheless, the code-breakers went to work. There were dozens of them, all over Europe, in Britain, in the United States. Inevitably they got some of their translations all balled up; they made a few crash landings in the highlands of etymology, and they got into unbecoming fights with each other. Most of them were geniuses.

The first man into the fray along with Missionary Wright was a young Welsh scholar named Archibald Henry Sayce. He too was a clergyman, and he had an astonishing flair for languages. At ten he had read Virgil and Homer in the original; at eighteen he had learned Hebrew, Egyptian, Persian, and Sanskrit. When the whole Hittite controversy began, he was called in to arbitrate and he declared himself on the side of Wright: the mysterious writing on the Hamath stones was Hittite, he said. In addition to the Biblical references, he based his conclusions on some strange sculptures that had turned up in Carchemish, on the right bank of the Euphrates River near the Syrian border with Turkey. These in turn resembled some rock carvings near modern Izmir, in Turkey, and some others far off to the north of Turkey near a village called Boghazkoy. All, Sayce decided, were Hittite. Further, he remembered having read in a German scientific journal something about a little silver plaque that had the picture of what appeared to be a king and some strange cuneiform writing on it. Sayce went off to the British Museum to see what was known there about this silver plaque or seal. The Museum had indeed once had it, but had decided it was a fake because nothing like it had ever been seen before. Before rejecting the seal, however, the Museum had prudently made a metal impression of it. Sayce was given this little reproduction to examine, and he made a brilliant discovery: not only was the king Hittite, according to Sayce, and not only did the little seal have an outer rim of cuneiform writing, as the Germans had said. But also its inner

The inscriptions on this stone, the base of an honorary stele found in the ruins of Ephesus, are Greek, in different styles of writing. The letters on the left face belong to the late Roman period, although they are written in Greek. On the right face, the upper half is a Greek inscription of the early Byzantine period, while the lower section is a later one belonging to the late Byzantine. The inscriptions of different periods carved on the same stone are just one of the difficulties encountered by the code-breakers.

A massive Hittite carving stands on a cliffside just east of Izmir, at a place called Karabel. It is badly weathered but immensely dramatic, and was one of the early clues to the enormous geographical spread of the Hittites during their days of glory.

circle had a hieroglyphic or ideogram writing just like that of the Hamath stones.

Loud hoots of laughter greeted Sayce at this point, and he was lampooned as the "inventor" of the Hittites.

Sayce defended himself brilliantly by pointing out that Assyrian sources spoke often of the "Land of the Hatti" (or "Chatti" —it could be read either way), and that Egyptians went on and on about their battles with the "Heta" or "Kheta" people. In fact, the longest of all the long-winded Egyptian inscriptions about Pharaonic victories was one Rameses II had had carved on a temple at Thebes to commemorate his victory over the Hittites at Kadesh, on the Orontes River.

In pursuit of his passion, Parson Sayce stormed all over the Middle East looking for inscriptions, sculptures, rock carvings. He turned up in Turkey; he had himself lowered with ropes for close looks at blurred, weathered cliff writings. Through all this he never discarded his dignified clerical dress. The natives called him "the gentleman with the swallow's tail," or "the crazy priest."

Yet it was another, later man who cracked the code of Hittite cuneiform and who made the startling, almost incredible discovery that the Hittite language was not Eastern but Indo-European —a member of the whole group of languages spoken in India, in western Asia, and in most of Europe. A modern traveler jetting across one border after another may become unhinged by the diversity of modern languages, but in many key words there is a revealing similarity. The modern English "father," for example, is clearly kin to the Latin *pater,* the Greek *patér,* even the Sanskrit *pitar*—to say nothing of the current French *père,* the Italian and Spanish *padre,* and the German *Vater.*

The word that provided the clue to the Indo-European nature of Hittite was the simple one "eat." A young scholar named Friedrich (Bedřich) Hrozný found it just before the outbreak of World War I. Hrozný was not, like so many of the great codebreakers, a clergyman. He was the son of one, however, born in Bohemia (now part of Czechoslovakia) in 1879. His father wanted him to be a minister, and while dutifully studying Protestant theology, young Hrozný became interested in the ancient

Orient and in Oriental languages. He was on his way, and in due course he came head on into the strange cuneiform writing of the Hittites.

He began, as all students of unknown languages begin, by trying to make out forms that looked familiar because they were known in other languages. With the aid of hieroglyphics or ideograms, he deciphered "fish" and "father" and some proper names. Gradually, because of some sentence structures, he began to have a nagging feeling that maybe, just maybe, Hittite was Indo-European. If it was, of course, most of the historians of the Near East would have been proved wrong. But so little was known yet, after all, of the Hittites. Hrozný shoved the idea to the back of his head and kept on working.

Then one day he came across a sentence which, rendered into the Roman alphabet, read, *Nu, ninda-an ezzateni watar-ma ekuteni.* (There are several scholarly spellings of this important sentence, this one as acceptable as the others.) The only word Hrozný recognized for sure was the second one, *ninda*, which he could deduce because its symbol was similar to a Sumerian or Babylonian ideogram for the same word. It meant "bread." As he pondered the sentence, Hrozný decided it would be logical that one of the words should mean "eat." He stared hard at the word *ezzateni*, and he thought. In Latin, "to eat" was *edere*; in Greek, *edein.* He grabbed a piece of paper and wrote down the words. Then he thought of High German, which he knew well: the word "to eat" was *ezzan*. Hrozný didn't even take time, apparently, to shout that triumphant cry of the ages, "Eureka!" He was too excited. If the first words of the sentence said "bread" and "eat," then wouldn't it be logical that the second half might say "water" and "drink"? There was that word *watar*, so close to the English "water," to the German *Wasser.* . . .

From this point on, Hrozný applied his Indo-European theory to all the Hittite texts he could lay his hands on. Usually it worked, though he also encountered many a borrowed word from Eastern and Semitic sources. He published a preliminary report in 1915 and another, definitive, one in 1917. It was one of the most detailed, complete decipherments of a dead language that had ever been handed to the world in one gulp, and it bore a formidable title: *The Language of the Hittites: Its Structure and Its Membership in the Indo-European Linguistic Family.*

The book not only electrified the savants; it also, by a strange quirk of fate, brought immortality to an otherwise totally unknown Austrian army lieutenant. It happened like this: Young Hrozný was deep in his studies when World War I broke out. There was little exemption for scholars in those days, and Hrozný was drafted. But he was drafted into the Austro-Hungarian army, and he fell under the command and into the hands of a friendly lieutenant. The lieutenant may not have understood a thing Hrozný was babbling about, but something impressed him, and he thoughtfully released his young draftee from as much military duty as possible. He even helped Hrozný get permission to go off to Constantinople to study inscriptions in the museum there, and to continue his work. The result was that in the preface to this first monumental work on the ancient language of the Hittites there is specific thanks to one "Lieutenant A. Kammergruber" for his "understanding consideration of the author's work."

6

THE HITTITE HABITAT

In the past twenty-five years, the reborn Hittites have become the darlings of the amateur archaeologist and the tourist. Many go to Turkey just to see the ruins of their great shrines and cities, and even when they've seen the famous ones they want to see more.

Never, for example, in all the books I had read about Hittites had I ever noticed the name Ivriz. Then in the late summer of 1970, in the Istanbul Archaeological Museum, I saw an enormous carved rock relief which fascinated me. It looked 20 feet high, and on it a most majestic god, festooned with grapes, was receiving homage from a small but beguiling king who appeared to be standing on a rock and who wore the typical Hittite turned-up shoes.

Museum attendants, answering my excited questions, said this was "only a copy." The real one was still in place at a town called Ivriz, near Konya, far to the south and east. Even the original, they said a bit snootily, was only "neo-Hittite, or late Hittite, about the middle of the eighth century B.C." Never mind; for me it was love at first sight. In my mind, little Ivriz had just been promoted to a major Hittite habitat. Besides, I wasn't sure exactly where it was or how to get there, so the element of discovery was injected instantly.

My Nemrud Dagh companion and I set forth for Ivriz from the town of Nevsehir, in central Turkey. The road went mostly west, skirting some of the high, snow-covered peaks of the Taurus mountain range and swinging below the white salt sea the Turks call Tuz Golu. There's hardly any water in the sea—just a vast, eerie plain of crystalline salt. We had by now acquired two guidebooks, and both said that to get to Ivriz one should proceed to Eregli, then turn south. Before Eregli, the sun vanished and a pounding rain drummed on the car. Eregli looked fascinating, with crumbling fortifications and what appeared to be canals but may have been only overflowing drains, in the downpour. Eregli is very old: it was captured by Arabs in A.D. 806, and in 1101 two columns of Crusaders on their way to the Holy Land were waylaid and destroyed here. It fell to an Armenian king of Cilicia in 1211, and to the Mongols in 1234.

We didn't stop: historic Eregli demanded of us this day only a decision. The 1960 guidebook said that Ivriz was 19 miles from here and that one should hire a guide. The 1969 guidebook said that Ivriz was "about a six-mile drive, plus two miles on foot or by muleback." We decided to believe 1969 and to do without the guide. We also decided to do the last 2 miles on foot. Memories of that mule ride up Nemrud Dagh were still too painfully fresh in our minds. And other places. There were no signs to Ivriz, but there seemed to be only one main road, so we took it. Then with a flash the sun burst through the rain, the road forked sharply, and one fork was marked "Ivriz." A sign from heaven, sure as anything, just like those meteors over Hama.

The road was very narrow, no more than 10 feet wide, and very bumpy, but there were slim and lovely poplars along both sides, and neat little houses back off the road, and two-wheeled carts full of apples, with apple-cheeked men and women jogging along behind the horses. They waved and smiled, in friendly Turkish fashion. We came to a fork, then another fork, neither marked. I looked at the mileage gauge: we had done more than the 6 miles advertised in 1969's guide. The road got narrower, and we passed a dam and a hydraulic project. This, I decided, would be the beginning of the 2-mile walk. But there was no village. The road lurched on, so we lurched with it. We slithered through ominous mudholes, around hairpin turns, and suddenly there was a village. It was eerily deserted, silent. Small, neat houses faced a pounded-earth main street; the street itself threatened to end at each curve and corner. Finally I spotted an old lady leaning over a wall, 10 feet above me. I got out of the car and delivered a solemn gesture somewhere between a wave and a salaam, hoping it would look polite, and inquired if this village was Ivriz. She said it was. But how to ask for directions to the Hittite rock relief? I whipped out one of the guidebooks, found a photograph of it, and held out the book. The old lady looked blank and then, to spare either her feelings or mine, she absolutely vanished from the wall.

As I was getting back into the car, around the corner came a man with a donkey. The donkey stepped daintily along under a load of apple-filled baskets, and the man looked politely curious. From him I inquired if this was Ivriz, and he said, *"Evet"*—yes. Then I showed him the picture in the guidebook, and he smiled and pointed straight ahead. Farther on *that* road? We went on.

Only about 60 yards farther, the road plunged over a little hill and collapsed on the edge of a stream. There was an enormous tree at water's edge, and we pulled the car in under it and looked around. Small but rugged cliffs shot straight up on the far side of the stream, and behind them were the tumbled hills of a low range of mountains. Were those ruins or just rocks, jumbled there together? The stream itself was littered with big boulders, the biggest of which had freshly washed Turkish carpets draped over them to dry. Trees hung well over the water on our side. Suddenly I spotted a Turkish schoolboy, in his black military-cut jacket and cap, looking at us silently. Grabbing my trusty guidebook, I showed *him* the picture of the rock relief, and he pointed very calmly to the other side of the stream. Pretty cool, I thought, for a native about to send two foreigners on a two-hour hike into those rocky cliffs. *"Merci,"* I told him, having discovered that the French word for "Thank you" will do quite as well as the hopelessly complicated Turkish *Cok tesekkur ederim*.

Carefully we loaded a rucksack with a thermos of mineral water, the lightest of the guidebooks, both our cameras, sunglasses, raisins, and as many of those Nemrud Dagh nuts as it would hold. Then we set forth, bravely, over the little bridge. I looked at my watch and at the sun, and said that I still thought we could make the trek before dark, if we didn't get lost.

To the right over the bridge we saw a little dam, and a neat gate which looked as if it led to the dam-keeper's cottage—and 20 yards behind the gate was the rock relief of Ivriz. Right there, before our eyes.

We stumbled forward almost in a trance, past the smiling mustached man in the neat brown uniform, past two children and an old man and a dog sleeping in the sun, and stopped 20 feet away from the carving to gasp. Whoever chose that rock on which to carve had chosen with consummate skill. It was an outcrop on the cliff which looked almost like a shell, so gently concave that its curve didn't distort the line of the carving, but just concave enough to protect it from the rain and the weather. The carving looked as crisp, as unblurred by time, as if it had stood for 27 years instead of 2,700. In the living rock, on the right, stood the little king, who was larger than life at about 6 feet, and facing him was that majestic god, 12 or 15 feet high. The Turks have put up a fence on the near side of a natural small ravine in front of the relief, to thwart that human urge to touch, and they had planted a few flowering shrubs well away from the carving but within the eye's range, to give it color. Otherwise it stands stark and simple, as it was meant to stand, with no plaques or explanations or translations of the hieroglyphic script carved near its base. The king has a richly embroidered short tunic, and turned-up shoes, and a curly beard. The god wears a tiara with horns, the horns a Hittite symbol for the ranks of their various gods. He holds in his left hand some ears of corn, and in his right a vine stock with leaves and grapes. He is a fertility god, and the homage-paying king is Warpalawas, a contemporary of the Assyrian King Tiglath Pileser III, who reigned about 800 B.C.

Scholars believe that Warpalawas ruled a small Hittite state in this region almost four centuries after the great Hittite empire fell in the north. Some of Warpalawas' ancestors had done battle with Tiglath Pileser III's ancestors, but now the Hittites' power was broken, and they lived on in lesser states in pockets of the old empire or farther south and east in regions that they had once

The great rock carving at Ivriz, near Eregli, dating from the second half of the eighth century B.C., shows the god of fertility, left, receiving a salute of homage from King Warpalawas, at right.

conquered. Warpalawas' own capital is believed to have been a few miles north and east of Ivriz, and the choice of this particular site for the great rock relief is a matter of conjecture. It stands near a spring which may have provided water for the fields of the little Hittite kingdom and which may even have been credited in that day with magic or curative powers. Certainly a resource as important as water would have been worth the attention both of the god of fertility and of the reigning king. I like to think that the site itself, in the rugged cliffs with the comforting gurgle of the stream at its feet, may have been irresistible to the artist.

It was difficult to turn around, at last, and walk away from the great rock relief. I felt foolishly that I should have backed away, as from the presence of royalty, but I would have felt even more foolish if, in so doing, I had inadvertently backed into the stream. As we drove back to the main road, the peasants burst out, from wherever they had been hiding, as suddenly as had the sun on the edge of Eregli. It was as if they had been waiting to see how we would react to their local treasure, and they matched our awe with their sudden friendliness. Each time we halted the car, to let a woman cross with her donkey load of wood or nuts, or to let straining men finish loading the ancient produce trucks that blocked the narrow road, they ran to the car to offer walnuts through the open windows, and apples which they polished carefully on grimy trousers or clean rough shirts before handing them over, smiling. There was no longer the shred of a cloud in the sky, and no feeling of hurry whatever within the kingdom of Warpalawas and that benign fertility god.

Going to Boghazkoy, near the site of the great fortified city that was the capital of the Hittite Empire, is another thing entirely. Here a wide modern highway sweeps east and north out of bustling Ankara, headed for the Black Sea. The road is crowded with buses and trucks whose drivers are as fierce as any of their warlike ancestors who were the scourge of the West four hundred years ago. At Sungurlu the road to Boghazkoy goes to the right, along a wide, fertile valley, and then the mountains begin. The small streams fight through the rocks and meet at a gorge. Beside it stands the little Turkish town—and beyond it, behind it, sprawling over the craggy cliffs, are the ruins of great cyclopean walls, put together without mortar from rocks of irregular sizes and shapes. Once these walls enclosed a city of more than 300 acres on top of this rocky crag, a city as large as Athens at the height of its power. Massive masonry gateways open the great walls, guarded still by roaring lions with oddly curly hair. This once was Hattusas, capital of the Hittite Empire.

Three thousand years after it fell, it was reborn to the West through the eyes of an adventurous French traveler named Charles-Félix-Marie Texier. Texier hadn't the foggiest notion what he had found when he came upon Hattusas. The year was 1834. He traveled by caravan to Boghazkoy, and there the villagers told him of a ruined city on the hill. He climbed up to it and stopped, stunned by its size. When Texier first saw the ruins, one massive gate still had the figure of a man of superhuman size— perhaps a king or a god, he thought—with sturdy legs and rippling muscles and a curved short sword in his right hand. The carving was unlike anything Texier ever had seen before.

Desperately, he tried to fit these mysterious ruins into the context of a Roman ruin, a culture he knew. "I was inclined to take these ruins for a Temple of Jupiter," he wrote later, "but I found myself compelled to abandon this opinion. No edifice of any Roman era could be fitted in here. . . ."

Nor could anything else in the known world be fitted here: at this point in time only Sheik Ibrahim had written of the mysterious stones of Hamath. The name "Hittite" slept quietly in the Bible, and on the rock inscriptions in Egypt, and on the clay tablets of the Assyrians.

Texier had still another shock in store for him. After he had mentally measured off the size of the ruined city and made drawings of its massive gates, he let his Turkish guide lead him, stumbling and slipping, across a valley and up a rocky path to a plateau almost as high as the site of the ruined city. Here there was a natural cleft in the high walls. The stone of one wall had been smoothed, at about eye level, and across it marched a strange, stiff procession: male figures with short tunics, turned-up shoes, high pointed caps. Their costumes were belted at the waist, and they carried scimitars in their right hands. Dazed, Texier wan-

The great Lion Gate of the capital city of the Hittite Empire, Hattusas, which dates from 1750 B.C. The gates led into the inner, fortified section of the walled city. The head of the lion at left has been broken off.

dered deeper into the cleft in the rock, into a gallery open to the sky. Here were larger figures wearing tiaras instead of pointed caps. Some stood on the backs of animals or of kneeling human figures; two were winged.

Facing this scene, as if passing the whole enigmatic procession in review, was the largest relief in the gallery. It showed a male figure in a long robe, turned-up shoes, and a close-fitting skullcap, with a strange curving symbol in his left hand. Not far from him was an exquisite rock carving of two male figures. The small one, dressed exactly the same as the giant figure, was held in the embrace of a much taller figure wearing a short tunic and a tall conical tiara with six sets of symbolic "horns."

What had he found? Texier questioned his guide and learned only that the Turks called the place "Yazilikaya," which means "inscribed rock."

Later, when he published a thick book of his travels, Texier admitted that he was utterly baffled. So far as any historian knew at that moment, no people mighty enough to have built the ruined fortified city and the strange open-air shrine had ever existed in that part of Asia Minor.

There matters rested in the old Hittite capital for about seventy years. The alarm clock, however, was about to go off. The

Gods wearing conical hats and carrying scimitarlike swords seem to be moving to the right. Actually, they are standing still, archaeologists say; Hittite sculptors never carved front views of figures, so they lined up these gods in profile.

Hamath and Aleppo stones were being deciphered; some Englishmen found the Mound of Carchemish on a bend in the Euphrates just over the present Turkish border with Syria; a pioneer Turkish archaeologist found some strange sculptures in a place called Zinjirli nearby; a Frenchman turned up some cuneiform tablets near Boghazkoy in 1893–94; and antique dealers in Ankara, Turkey, suddenly had for sale in 1880 some curious tablets which came, they said, from a mound of ruins known as Kultepe.

By the dawn of the twentieth century, the code-breakers and the archaeologists were sure they were hot on the trail of the Hittites. A British expedition promoted by Archibald Henry Sayce, the man who only shortly before had "invented" the Hittites, went off in 1906 to dig near Boghazkoy, to search for more physical proof of the existence of this nation whose story was emerging. Not until they were well on their way did they get the surprising news that their permission to dig had been withdrawn, and that instead they were to be sent off to Carchemish to explore what seemed to be a "late Hittite" site. This sudden switch snatched from the aging Sayce and his fellow British archaeologists the honor of digging at last in the great ruins that were to prove all their theories correct. Instead, that honor went to a German expedition under Dr. Hugo Winckler. The reason for the switch was political; in 1906 Turkey was still ruled by a Sultan, and the reigning one, Abdul-Hamid II, was more impressed by the belligerent Kaiser Wilhelm than he was by Britain's King Edward VII. The Kaiser fancied himself a patron of archaeology, and so the Sultan handed to the Kaiser's men the plum of the Boghazkoy dig.

Winckler was by all accounts a cantankerous fellow who sat in his tent sweating and slapping at bugs and feverishly decoding clay tablets and cuneiform inscriptions while the diggers hacked away. His expeditions found a treasure in tablets, however—more than ten thousand of them, in what must have been the Hittite palace archives.

Suddenly the names of the Hittite kings emerged from the shadows, and the dates of their reigns could be worked out. There were codes of law, and clay-tablet "letters" to allies and friends, and business transactions. On one wonderful day, decipherers made out the Hittite version of a treaty between Egypt's Pharaoh Rameses II and the Hittite King Hattusilis III, an "everlasting peace" signed sometime between the years 1280 and 1269 B.C. One version of this treaty had been carved into a temple at Karnak on the Nile, in Egyptian hieroglyphics. Now here, suddenly, was the Hittite copy, in the archives of the capital city of Hattusas. There could be no further doubt of the power of the Hittites during the great days of their empire.

To all except the dedicated scholar and the professional linguist or archaeologist, the endless chronicles of long-dead kings and their correspondence can be soporific after five minutes. Yet out of the palace archives of Hattusas came the strange saga of an appealing warrior king, and the sad story of a youthful Queen of Egypt whose piquant plight comes yearning across the millennia. . . .

The king was Suppuliumas I, and he reigned from 1375 to 1335 B.C., when the empire was still very strong. A talented warrior, he was also renowned as an arranger of high-level marriages: he would conquer a country and then make it an ally by marrying one of his relatives to the royal house of the conquered country. He finally led his rampaging charioteers and scimitar-swingers all the way south from his mountain capital to the borders of the present nation of Lebanon, and then he withdrew, back across the Euphrates River near Carchemish, to rest.

While he and his army were camped there, a messenger arrived from Egypt carrying one of those little baked-clay-tablet "letters" to King Suppuliumas. It purported to be from the Queen of Egypt, and it read, "My husband has died, and I have no son. Of you it is said that you have many sons. If you would send me one of your sons, he could become my husband. I will on no account take one of my subjects and make him my husband. *I am very much afraid.*" (Italics are the author's.)

Suppuliumas, who was old then and possibly tired of his thirty years of war and political matchmaking, carried the letter back to Hattusas with him, but he did not save copies of his replies to the frightened queen. She wrote him again, in further tablets found at Hattusas. "Why do you say, 'They are deceiving me?'" she asked the Hittite king. "If I had a son, would I write to a foreigner to publish my distress and that of my country? You have insulted me in speaking thus. . . ."

In the end, Suppiluliumas did send one of his sons to Egypt, but the prince never got there. What happened to him, and to the queen, can only be surmised by careful dating and study of Egyptian records, laws, and customs. The best theory seems to be that the queen, probably no more than sixteen years old, was Ankheshamen, child bride of the Pharaoh Tutankhamen, the famous "King Tut" whose tomb was discovered in Egypt in 1922. When her young husband died, the girl queen was at the mercy of all the swarm of nobles, priests, courtiers vying for the vacant throne. It was Egyptian custom that the only way for the next Pharaoh to take over legitimately was to marry the widow. Either Queen Ankheshamen must have had a fairly good idea which of the warring courtiers would win (and decided she didn't want him for a husband), or else she thought to pull off a coup by wedding one of the sons of the great Hittite house and thus making herself one of the most powerful queens in history. Whichever it was, it didn't work. Somebody murdered the young would-be bridegroom on his way to Thebes, and the list of Egyptian kings shows that the next Pharaoh after Tut was an elderly man named Ay, who had been a chief minister at the Egyptian court.

Poor young Hittite prince, and poor young queen . . . their sad story was deciphered too late to provide a plot for Shakespeare; but how could writers of the raging melodrama of grand opera have missed them as subjects?

Behind Winckler and his tablet-hunters at Boghazkoy came a patient, thoughtful archaeologist of another stripe, another German named Kurt Bittel. He too found tablets, but what he had uppermost in mind was to reconstruct the ancient citadel and its life in the minds of men. For years he dug, aided by the Turks, and slowly the size of Hattusas emerged, something of the life of its people and their gods.

The Egyptians' pictorial representations of their enemies the Hittites made them look most unattractive: stocky, hook-nosed, clad in long garments which led some scholars to opine that perhaps it was the fierce Hittites, in their long skirts, who accounted for that persistent Near Eastern legend of the Amazons, the female warriors.

In the Hittites' representations of themselves they don't look much more handsome. They show themselves as short and stocky, enormous-nosed, broad-shouldered, and clad mostly in no-nonsense woolen robes and sturdy, turned-up boots—which must have been very practical indeed for the climate in the Turkish mountains that were their central homeland. They were clever military architects, wrapping their Cyclopean walls around mountain fastnesses, and they worked out one of the most humane law codes of the ancient world. They did not believe in "an eye for an eye," and they spelled out careful instructions for the treatment of conquered peoples. Like almost all of their contemporaries, they had slaves and they expected others to have them, but their law code specifically extended justice to slaves as well as freemen: a Hittite king instructs his commanders, when they enter a city, "If the slave of a man or the maidservant of a man has a suit, decide it for them and satisfy them. . . . Do what is just."

As a rough, mountain folk they did not create delicate and sophisticated works of art, though they were masters of the massive and their great rock reliefs have compelling power. They made handsome monochrome pottery and specialized in a long-snouted jug whose form still exists today, in metal, in the bazaars of modern Turkey. They had iron and worked it with such success that the Pharaohs write letters to them begging for this precious product. In the days of the Hittites, iron was much more expensive than gold because of its military value it was probably forty times as dear as silver.

Between wars they seem to have lived well, by their own record: they showed themselves slightly paunchy and contented, surrounded by symbols of corn and grapes, and in few reliefs of the ancient world is there such a constant happy presence of children and animals.

They had a swarm of gods, whom they apparently worshiped in open-air shrines and customarily pictured as larger than life. Many they had merely adopted from other peoples and other lands—a sea god who may have originated in Sumer, a goddess

This tunnel, more than 220 feet long, enabled defenders of the city to slip out secretly and attack the enemy from the rear. The tunnel was a central defense point beneath another city gate, the Sphinx Gate, and could be blocked at both ends so that enemies could not see it.

An inner view of the long tunnel, showing how it was constructed of huge boulders with no concrete or other binding.

A carving typical of the late Hittite period in southern Turkey shows the customary lion with snarling open mouth, and a magic beast, half man and half animal, at right. The carving, which comes from the area of Zincirli and dates from about 750–700 B.C., is now in the Archaeological Museum of Istanbul.

Beautifully made terra-cotta bulls, about 18 inches high, were painted red and white, and date from about 1700–1600 B.C. They were found in the ruins of the Hittite capital, Hattusas (present-day Boghazkoy).

A bronze stag about 6 inches high, not counting his antlers, was used as a ritual standard on top of a lance. It is Hittite, from the site of Alacahüyük, and dates from the second half of the third millennium B.C.

of love derived from the one of Mesopotamia, a moon god, a god of grain, a sun god. But the most important god of their pantheon was Teshub the weather god. Mighty Teshub is in some details the forerunner of the familiar Olympian Zeus, as he is often shown standing in sturdy lonely majesty, clutching a bolt of symbolic lightning in one hand and an ax in the other. His symbolic animal was the bull. One of the most enormous structures excavated at Hattusas (more than 500 feet by 400 feet) was the temple of the weather god, a complex of nine rooms containing places of worship, a series of storerooms for food and oil and wine, and an open court in which the figure of the god himself must once have stood. No free-standing statue of him has ever been found, nor has any other cult statue of the early Hittites. Did they never sculpt proper statues, or did unknown hands carry them away? Archaeologists don't know. The only gods to remain today are those carved into the great rock reliefs.

Yazilikaya, that maze of hand-carved ancient rock into which Texier wandered with such wonder in 1834, was the national sanctuary of the Hittite Empire, a natural formation turned into a shrine by representations of the Hittite gods. There are so many of them that archaeologists are still trying to sort out which is which, but some are identifiable. The largest gallery, they believe, was created during the reign of Hattusilis III (1275–1250 B.C.). The enormous king figure that dominates the gallery probably represents his son Tudhaliya, who later ruled with his mother, and the fine relief of the giant god embracing the king is believed to be the god Sharruma embracing this same Tudhaliya in a gesture signifying honor and protection.

Despite their great power, at least some of the Hittite gods had most appealing human characteristics. There is one myth about a god called Telepinus who flew into a terrible rage one day and shouted, "There must be no interference!" And then, the myth says, he got so excited that he tried to put his right shoe on his left foot and his left shoe on his right foot. The description is enough to give the most terrified believer the giggles, but unfortunately the tablet on which it is inscribed is broken off just at the point where one might have learned just what Telepinus was so mad about.

The most recently excavated part of the ancient city, this is a store-room of a temple of the Weather God. No representation of the god has been found at Hattusas, but it was customary to store immense amounts of food and drink in the huge temples.

Probably the most beautiful relief in the entire sanctuary of Yazilikaya, this carving shows King Tudhaliya (1250–1220 B.C.), clutching a kal-mush, the sign of sovereignty in his left hand, and being held in an embrace by the god Sharruma. This was the embrace of honor and protection. The god's headdress has symbolic horns, signifying his rank, and he wears a short kiltlike garment, while the king wears a long robe. Both have the typical Hittite turned-up shoes.

A group of Turkish children try to drive a wandering steer out of the Hittite sanctuary at Yazilikaya. On the wall behind them is the central group of the gods, the main scene in the sanctuary. At left, standing on two mountains, is the great Hittite Weather God of Heaven. Facing him is his consort, the goddess Hepat, known also as the Sun Goddess of Arinna, here standing on a panther. Behind her is her son, the god Sharruma, who is standing on a smaller panther.

Then suddenly, about 1180 B.C., the record stops. There are no more tablets in Hattusas, no additional rock carvings at Yazili-kaya. So great was the catastrophe that even the Hittite tradition vanished from Central Anatolia and from the memories of men. All that survived was small kingdoms, little settlements, off on the fringes of the once-great empire; and these, of course, were the unimportant-sounding tribesmen encountered by the Biblical Abraham and King David. There are even echoes of the Hittite style and customs on Nemrud Dagh, in the tablets of King Anti-ochus being embraced by *his* pantheon of gods, as late as the first century before Christ. But the empire was gone and the thread was broken in some cataclysm which archaeologists have not yet fully explained. Some Assyrian records mention a people from eastern Europe who overran the area about that period. Homer's Troy could have fallen to them, according to the dates. Egyptian sources agree that about this same time there was a massive inva-sion of "sea people." These invaders, still not clearly identified, apparently came in boats from the west, across the Mediterra-nean, and may have been early Etruscans, Sardinians, Sicilians.

The ruins of Hattusas show that the city died by fire, in a roar-ing conflagration which may have lasted for days or even weeks. Did the city's destroyers take away with them the missing cult statues, the royal treasure? These things have never turned up in the ruins. Nobody knows yet. There is just a sudden silence in Anatolia, and the inscription on an Egyptian temple wall which says that when the "sea people" came "no land held fast before them."

7

WHO OWNS THE PAST?

One very hot day I was standing in the ruins of Pergamum, in western Turkey, trying to get up enough courage to take a picture of the most frightening theater I have ever seen. Its hand-hewn rock seats went straight down the side of a cliff and vanished into a valley. There were no guardrails. The guidebook assured me that when the Greeks had built the theater a couple of thousand years ago it offered an "unhampered view of the stage." Unhampered indeed. Any first-nighter headed for his seat must have been in imminent danger of arriving on the stage, totally unhampered by ticket, costume, or any knowledge of what he should say when he bounced into the middle of a scene.

In its day, this magnificent stabilized landslide could seat fifteen thousand persons. The acoustics, say the experts, were perfect. Impressed but queasy, I turned back toward the rocky hillside and scrambled upward. Within minutes I arrived at an enormous heap of tumbled stone which partially blocked the view of some handsome marble columns. Stuck into the heap of stones was a neat sign in four languages (Turkish, German, English, and French, in that order) which said sternly, "No Entry."

No entry? The sign should have been at the theater. But its

A steeply built Greek theater survives in the ruins of Pergamum.

The "No Entry" sign marks only jumbled heaps of marble.

message was clear. What it really said was "Keep out of our price-less ruins and please don't steal the columns."

Who really owns that ancient theater, and the columns, and the heap of ruined rock? Who owns the buried cities and the marble heads and the broken pots? The people who made them—the Hittites or the Phrygians, the classical Greeks and the imperial Romans, the Lydians or the Urartians—will not come again to claim them.

From the dawn of history until almost our own era, the ruins and the treasures belonged quite simply to whoever got there first. It was neither a philosophical question nor a pragmatic one. In the beginning it was a matter of simple survival. As one tribe followed another one, or as one civilization conquered its prede-cessor, the human survivors simply took over the territory and used whatever was on it. Thus Hittites built on pre-Hittite ruins, and Phrygians built on Hittite ruins. Each used the others' stone and bits of wall, wells and fields. Sometimes they used the old pots; sometimes they even saved the old statues. Good ideas thought up by one people were often borrowed by others, or adapted to local conditions.

This very Pergamum where I stood that day was founded in the mists of prehistory. Then it became Greek. Then it was Roman, and now it is a ruin. When Pergamum was Roman, it housed one of the great libraries of the ancient world, an institu-tion so famous that it annoyed the Egyptians, because they con-sidered that they had the greatest library in the civilized world at the city of Alexandria, on the mouth of the Nile. Egypt became in fact so distressed at the idea of an upstart city like Pergamum having a great library that she cut off all supplies of papyrus, the primitive writing material that was made from the pulp of an Egyptian water plant. When papyrus vanished from the market, the people of Pergamum invented *carta pergamena*, "the paper of Pergamum," made from the cured skins of goats and sheep. From this invention came their great library and our word "parchment." Even then the battle of the libraries wasn't over, however: The Roman Julius Caesar burned up the library in Alexandria, and this mightily offended Cleopatra, the Queen of Egypt. So Cleopatra's friend Mark Antony took two hundred

The site of Pergamum as it looks today, with the Meander River (now known as the Menderes) visible in the background. In ancient times Pergamum was on the sea. Since then the river has silted, creating a land basin between the sea and the hill on which the city was built.

thousand parchments from the library in Pergamum and gave them to Cleopatra to restock Alexandria's shelves. Then, four hundred years later, the Arabs burned the library in Alexandria again, and all the precious parchments were lost.

And so it went, through all the centuries. Always there were writers, painters, dreamers who mooned over the ruined cities and wrote of their stirring days. The painters faithfully recorded the sights of the great ruins. But most of the people who lived in or near them were notably unmoved. They dug up the old worked stones to build houses for themselves. They smashed marble statues to melt into lime, and they casually knocked inscriptions off old rocks because they couldn't read the words. It didn't happen only in Turkey: Italian peasants through the centuries battered Greek and Roman statues into pieces to build roads or make lime; Egyptians threw precious treasures at invading foreigners as if they were hurling rocks; Mongol invaders in the Middle East tore down temples to dam streams.

The message is clear: people, just ordinary ignorant people, are forever making an archaeological nuisance of themselves.

"If the field archaeologist had his will, every ancient capital would have been overwhelmed by the ashes of a conveniently adjacent volcano," once remarked the great British archaeologist Sir Leonard Woolley. Sir Leonard was being neither heartless nor jocular. What he meant was that a convenient volcano could so bury a city that immediately succeeding generations would have no chance to "mine" its walls or to break up its monuments. Ruined Pompeii in Italy, damaged though it was by early treasure hunters, remains today one of the most perfectly preserved of all ancient sites because Mt. Vesuvius erupted and buried it under tons of ash, where it lay undisturbed for almost 1,800 years.

When the world began to take an interest in its own past, in the eighteenth and nineteenth centuries, there were no "No Entry" signs on the ruins. Any spirited traveler of those days could poke about under the weeds and rocks and help himself to the artifacts. They were considered simply treasure, and treated as such. They belonged to the first and/or most skillful treasure hunter on the scene. Among the most daring and energetic of these early ruin-lovers were the British and the Germans, and they filled the museums of their nations with the remnants of the past.

Perhaps the best-known of all these casually looted treasures are the so-called Elgin Marbles in the British Museum in London. These include the magnificently carved marble reliefs of the fifth century B.C. that once decorated the Parthenon in Athens. A Scottish millionaire and art lover named Lord Elgin took them from Athens in the nineteenth century, with the full permission of Athens' Turkish rulers, and transported them by ship to Britain. As a minor footnote to quite another history, it is interesting that among Lord Elgin's companions and fellow explorers was a young scholar and linguist who was later to become famous as Lawrence of Arabia.

The Elgin Marbles caused a sensation when they were shown to the British public, and they set off a revolution in the art world. They also inspired in thousands of people a love for antiquity which may have helped save many another ancient monument.

Lord Elgin and his companions on these early antiquities crusades truly felt, with much justice, that they were saving the past for the rest of the world. In our era world travel is commonplace, and many a visitor to modern Athens longs to see the great marble reliefs *in situ* on the Parthenon; but a century ago such excursions were limited to the rich, and the only way ordinary people could admire ancient art was in public museums. Besides which, certain knowledge of the history of the Parthenon is enough to explain the actions of Lord Elgin: built originally as a temple to the pagan goddess Athena, the great Parthenon was converted into a church in the Middle Ages, and into a mosque when invading Turks captured Athens. So massive and so solid that it survived these transformations with little damage, the building was blown up in 1687 when Venetian troops attacked the Turks in Athens. The Turks had turned the Parthenon into a powder room, and when a Venetian shell hit it it went up in thunderous smoke, destroying almost everything except two pediments. By the time Lord Elgin came upon the remnants, two hundred years later, he felt that the only way to save what was left was to take it to relatively peaceful England. Greek soldiers of his era, on guard on the towering Acropolis where the Parthenon stands, whiled away the boring hours by shooting noses and fingers off remaining statues and reliefs.

In the twentieth century, the whole picture changed. Tourism became a major industry. A great part of the affluent world was eager to see the ancient sites, and newly responsible governments in the old countries determined to keep their treasures instead of selling them or bargaining them away to persuasive foreigners with omnivorous museums. As always, the world divided itself into the haves and the have-nots. In this particular case, the "have" nations were such traditionally poor ones as Turkey, Greece, Italy, Syria, Egypt, and in our own hemisphere Mexico, Guatemala, Peru. The "have-nots," for once, were the United States, Britain, Germany, Switzerland . . .

The "haves" decided to defend themselves, and all of them framed laws forbidding illegal excavations and the sale abroad of pieces of antiquity. Turkey actually moved rather belatedly and ineffectually. Until after World War I it was ruled by a Moslem oligarchy which cared very little for the artifacts of the alien, invading world of Greece and Rome. The Ottoman rulers made deals with the English kings and German Kaisers for the transport of Greco-Roman remains. There is hardly a trace left of the two of the famous Seven Wonders of the ancient world that once stood in Turkey. One of these was the tomb of King Mausolus (Chapter 4), who ruled 375 years before Christ from a rocky promontory reaching into the extreme eastern shore of the Mediterranean in a town called Bodrum. Mausolus married his sister Artemis, and when he died his sister/widow commissioned the grandest tomb the world had ever seen. India's famous Taj Mahal, probably today's most celebrated tomb, was built in the 1600s, almost two thousand years later. King Mausolus' tomb was called the Tomb of Halicarnassus when it was built, taking its name from the royal city, but it has come down to us as the word "mausoleum." Alexander the Great destroyed it, and the Crusaders used some of its stones to build a fortress. A century ago, British diggers found and took away the statues and big frieze (a sculptured stone decorative band) that once adorned it. Today

This marble carving was once part of the frieze of the Mausoleum of Halicarnassus, the tomb of King Mausolus. It depicts a struggle between Greeks and Amazons, and the tomb that it once adorned was one of the Seven Wonders of the Ancient World.

only one small marble relief remains in the local museum to indicate the beauty of the ancient carving.

The second of the Seven Wonders in Turkey was the temple of the goddess Artemis, or Diana, in Ephesus, the magnificent city on the western shore of Turkey. Destroyed and rebuilt half a dozen times by invaders, it finally vanished, and its remaining artifacts were taken by British archaeologists to the British Museum in London. The great Frieze of the Temple of Jupiter from Pergamum is in East Berlin. The treasure of Troy was dug up by a German, taken to West Berlin, and allegedly stolen by the Russians in World War II. Enormous gate carvings from the Hittite capital of Hattusas have gone to foreign museums, and a Hittite rock carving near Izmir which had been seen and admired by travelers for two thousand years suddenly vanished in 1925 and has never been seen since.

"Of all the great source nations of antiquity, Turkey is the most plundered," said an American archaeologist recently. "Its casual destruction, by traders and treasure hunters, may be the *greatest scientific disaster of our century*." (Italics are the author's.)

These are strong words, but there is little doubt that they are true. Turkey has at least 3,000 already identified archaeological sites and more than 20,000 caves and mounds still unexcavated. Each year there are about 35 Turkish "digs" in progress and another 35 run by expeditions from foreign nations. In 1969 these legal and supervised excavations produced about 5,000 ancient objects—statues, vases, coins, sarcophagi—but in the same year the Turkish government bought almost 24,000 pieces from peasants who dug them up accidentally or illegally, and they confiscated almost 7,000 pieces that police found in the hands of those who had no right to have them. In an average year, Turkish officials estimate, 30,000 pieces of antiquity leave the country illegally, smuggled out by international traders who know that they can be sold to individuals or to museums for enormous sums of money. Relics of the past have become much in style in most of the world.

Turkish law on the matter is outdated, and the system for paying for treasure is confusing. The country's law against illegal excavation and traffic in "antiques" dates from 1906 and carries very light penalties: one year in jail and a fine of 10 Turkish lire, which is less than $1. A new law, raising jail sentences to five years and the fine to 10,000 Turkish lire, had not been passed at this writing, though all of the nation's museums and archaeologists were clamoring for it. Turkey has no police force specifically trained to spot genuine antiquities, and its busy law officers, like those of Italy, find it difficult to crack down on tomb robbers and antiquities traders in the face of more urgent matters like street violence and rioting students.

Only five years ago a British antiquities dealer, who admitted that he had sold several valuable pieces of pottery from Turkey to British museums, insisted that the pieces he handled had come "from a private Austrian estate near the Hungarian border." Ancient pots have no pedigree like that attached, say, to famous paintings, so when they vanish it is extremely difficult to prove exactly where they came from and which man in the long chain of dealers should be apprehended for theft or for trafficking. As early as 1938 some extremely valuable painted neolithic pottery (the word "neolithic" is an anthropological and geological term meaning toward the end of the Stone Age, before the Bronze Age —a date very roughly 6000 B.C. in Anatolia) was turning up for sale in Europe. Archaeologists and art historians could date this pottery and value it—and they valued it highly—but they had no clear idea where it came from. A great deal of it came from Turkey.

"The Turks at this time had no idea of value," said the same British dealer. "You could take a pot worth fifteen thousand dollars to any Turkish post office and mail it anywhere you wanted. The customs officers and postal officials and police were on the watch for gold. Anything that wasn't gold—well, that was okay, you could mail it abroad. The archaeologists knew, but they weren't at the post office."

After World War II, when the United States based thousands of troops in Turkey as part of the over-all NATO defense force for western Europe, U.S. Army Post Offices became handy exit points for illegally excavated statues, coins, pots. There was no Turkish customs control at an APO, and the GIs sent home hundreds of "souvenirs" not even knowing for sure what they sent.

The baggage of foreign diplomats was never checked, either, as they entered and departed from Turkey on official business. There have been dark charges in high Turkish government circles recently about diplomats with their bags stuffed full of antiquities.

A few years ago there was actual gunplay inside the archaeological museum in Izmir, Turkey, during a robbery, and a guard was killed. Turkish police captured a German citizen as he was leaving the country with the loot, though they never caught another German, a Yugoslav, and a Turk whom they described as his accomplices. The same year, another German "tourist" was halted in his car just because alert customs officials noticed that this was his twentieth visit to their country in one year. Doubting that any tourist would be quite that enthusiastic, they searched his car and found "hundreds" of antiquities tucked away in the trunk, beside the motor, under the seats.

In 1970 things came to a head in Turkey, however, in such an almighty uproar that it actually began to affect relations between the governments of Turkey and the United States. The fight began in Boston. In the spring of 1970, the Boston Museum of Fine Arts proudly opened a display of pre–Bronze Age jewelry, 137 pieces, of which most were pure gold. They came, the Museum said, from a royal tomb in "a Middle Eastern country" and they had been purchased in Switzerland by a patron of the Museum as a gift. No specific amount of money was ever mentioned, but talk of "six figures" made it clear that the hoard had cost at least $100,000. Instantly Turkey protested that *it* was the "Middle Eastern country" involved, and its archaeologists and diplomats asked, politely at first, just where and how the Museum had acquired this treasure from 3000 B.C. Boston officials said they did not know the precise provenance of the treasure, repeating only that it had been purchased in Switzerland. Since almost all of the illegally excavated antiquity from both Turkey and Italy eventually winds up in the hands of dealers in Switzerland, this explanation inflamed the Turks more than it pacified them. British archaeologist James Mellaart, asked to look at photographs of what became known as the "Boston hoard," said that it definitely was not the mysterious vanished "Dorak treasure" (Chapter 10).

The inspector general of the Greek archaeological service, whose country of course is "Middle Eastern" and therefore might have been the original provenance of the treasure, said that it was all "a grotesque forgery" presumably put together by unscrupulous dealers and sold in Switzerland. Dr. Emily Vermuele, a distinguished American archaeologist and wife of a director of the Boston museum, studied the 137 objects for two years before they went on display, and she pronounced them genuine Bronze Age objects. In style, she said, they resemble work of the period from any number of Middle Eastern and Mediterranean nations. But the Turks remain convinced that they come from Turkey.

"I believe that the Boston pieces come from sites in Anatolia and near Troy," said Raci Temizer, the director of the stunningly beautiful and important Archaeological Museum of Ankara, Turkey. "We don't care about the intrinsic value of the gold itself. You can buy gold in any jewelry store. But if these pieces are genuine, and I believe that some of them are, then they are a vital part of the story of ancient civilization in Anatolia, a civilization thousands of years older and more mysterious than, say, Greece or Rome. Once they have disappeared from the site in which they were found, much of their value disappears. Archaeologists must study these things *in situ*, relate them to their surroundings and to their period. Left there, they might provide vital clues to prehistory. When they are taken away, they become merely beautiful old things for people to look at."

Director Temizer, and many another Turkish scholar, also believe that the Metropolitan Museum in New York City has part of the legendary King Croesus' treasure from graves in western Turkey, and that Dumbarton Oaks in Washington has some illegally excavated Byzantine silver. An American businessman whom I met in Turkey, who has spent several years there, agrees with the Turks that the Metropolitan's treasure may indeed have belonged originally to King Croesus.

"I am known locally as a minor collector of the stuff you can buy here and keep as a personal collection so long as it doesn't leave the country," he told me. "Four or five years ago a peasant came to my office and told me that he and some friends had dug up 'a very good tumulus' near Sardis, which was King Croesus'

capital. The man had come to ask me how to contact international traders. Can you imagine being so naïve? I asked him if he
didn't know it was against the law. He said that didn't matter,
because the tumulus was way out in the country and anyway if
the *jandarma* [Turkish version of *gendarmes*, or police] turned
up, they'd just pay them off with part of the loot. I have no idea
what happened to it, but the location and the descriptions I have
read make me wonder if that isn't what the Metropolitan
bought."

Part of the problem is, of course, poverty. The Turkish peasant
farmer, scrambling for a living (annual mean income in Turkey
is $500 per year), has no particular enthusiasm for the intrinsic
beauty of the art forms of Greece and Rome so prized in the
West. So far as he can see, they have nothing to do with him. He
has even less comprehension of the much earlier art forms of his
native Anatolia, the Hittite or Phrygian. Why should he? Until
a man can read and write, and eat regularly, there is neither past
nor future. There is only today, and the demand of an empty
stomach.

"So long as American collectors and American museums have
one hundred dollars for a clay pot, and a Turkish peasant needs
one dollar to eat, the traffic will go on," said an American museum director. The difference between $1 and $100, of course,
goes to middlemen and to bribing any official who appears to be
bribable.

Every early traveler and excavator in the wilder reaches of
Anatolia has come home with tales of Roman inscriptions being
used as common doorsills, of Greek capitals upended to be used
as watering troughs for animals or hollowed out to make wine
presses. An American archaeologist working in Anatolia in 1929
told mournfully of having "tried for fully two hours to rescue a
Hittite stele, found a few weeks before, from its fate—being
crushed to gravel to be strewn on a new highway." Another time
he was forced to stand helplessly by and watch a large stone block
with a Greek inscription vanish as additional fill into a mass of
new concrete. The Turks of that era were totally baffled by his
concern, he said. "More than one old man patted me on the
shoulder with a benign smile, just as he would have patted a

A beautiful marble carving of soldiers is used to prop up the crumbling foundations of an ancient building in Istanbul.

child playing with a stone or a stick in which a grown-up can see nothing. But the younger men, less tolerant, smiled at me derisively, openly registering their convictions that I was mentally unsound."

The truth is that some peasants are canny and some are not. In the late nineteenth century, the German excavator Hugo Winckler was repeatedly offered clay tablets from a site near Kultepe, Turkey, and he became so interested that he interrupted his excavations at Hattusas to go dig near Kultepe. Mysteriously, he found nothing. Neither did two later expeditions to the same site. Not until early in the twentieth century was the mystery solved: the peasant farmers of Kultepe always helpfully pointed out to foreigners a huge mound from which they *said* they were taking the tablets. They were lying. They had actually found them in a smaller mound only a few hundred yards away, and they were digging them up on the sly, a few at a time, so as not to depress the market.

On a sunny day in April, 1970, Turkish engineers were working on a new road to Boghazkoy, a road designed to ease the journey of the growing number of tourists eager to see the Hittite habitat for themselves. Toward the end of the afternoon they were approached by a small delegation of farmers who asked if they could please borrow a bulldozer. The good-natured road builders, made even more amiable by the approach of quitting time, asked the farmers why they wanted a bulldozer. The vague answer was that they needed it "for an agricultural project."

Because the Turkish peasant is so clearly poverty-stricken, and the bulldozer such a delightful new toy for any man, the road builders expansively gave permission. At which point, under cover of darkness, the farmers promptly put the machine to work knocking the top off a small mound in the vicinity and making off with all the archaeological remains that hadn't been smashed in their rough approach.

Turkish archaeologists and officials rushed to the scene, when the word got out, and confiscated everything they could find— including a handsome statue of the goddess Cybele, the celebrated "Great Mother of the Gods," who was worshiped for centuries in this and other parts of the Near East.

"Those farmers wouldn't know Phrygian from Frigidaire," commented an observer of the untidy scene, "but they knew that stuff underground is valuable."

The abrupt approach is typical of the amateur or of the treasure hunter. Turkish policemen recently apprehended a student hidden in the ruins with a load of dynamite big enough to blow the temples and himself to kingdom come. He was only, the young man said, intending to "locate" the treasure in the temples. A British journalist told me that he was approached, a couple of years ago, by a farmer who had dug up a little classical gold statue. The farmer wanted to sell it, but the journalist declined, saying that he should take it to the museum. A few weeks later he saw the same farmer and asked how he had made out with his statue, and the man grinned and opened his mouth wide. Then he pointed to his gleaming, freshly capped gold teeth. The museum officials might have given him nothing for his gold, he explained. In fact, they would probably have taken it away. But now the treasure was his forever, in a form no policeman could ever confiscate.

Until four or five years ago, tourists in Turkey were offered bits of antiquity at all the major sites. It was even easier to kick around in the ruins and find your own. All that has stopped now in Turkey's desire to protect its own treasure. Two young Germans found standing in the ruins of Ephesus in the summer of 1970 with bits of carved stone in their hands were hustled abruptly off to the guardhouse to be questioned severely on their activities. Signs in all airports and customs sheds at boat landings admonish the visitor that antiquities may not be removed from the country. Usually a tourist caught with a coin, or a pot, or a small head, is permitted to go on his way, but the treasure he had had in his suitcase is summarily confiscated even if he had purchased it from an antique dealer.

Turkey's new vigilance is particularly trying for the dedicated men and women of the official "digs" that go on every year. Government permission to dig has always been required, and for years a resident Turkish archaeologist has been assigned to supervise every foreign crew in the field. But nowadays permissions come more and more slowly. Some expeditions have been blocked

In the great covered bazaar of Istanbul, merchants sell marble fragments, pots, and bits of ancient bronzes. Some are genuine, some not, but purchase of any one of them will make the unwary tourist subject to questioning at the airport, and possible confiscation of his souvenir.

in Ankara for weeks or even months waiting for permission to go on with their work.

The Turks are hopeful that "a new spirit of cooperation" will triumph and that the international traffic can be halted by peaceful means. They fought hard for an international agreement through the United Nations, and in November of 1970 a draft convention actually was approved in Paris at a meeting of UNESCO. The convention puts sixty-six signer nations on their honor to help restore stolen art and antiquity to its rightful nation, to combat theft from archaeological sites, and to oppose purchase of anything that has been stolen. The United States, pressured by its own archaeologists and students, reluctantly signed the convention, but has not ratified it. A year after the convention was agreed upon, only two nations, Ecuador and Bulgaria, had ratified it. There has been some moral effect, however: the Cleveland Museum let it be known that it had recently returned to Turkey a marble head which had left Turkey illegally and gone into the Cleveland Collection, and the University of Pennsylvania Museum announced that it would instantly halt purchase of any archaeological treasure which had illegally left its country of origin.

More U.S. museums are certain to add their voices to the clamor, because dozens of American schools of archaeology work in Turkey, and their permissions to continue are threatened by any lack of U.S. cooperation. The former Turkish Minister of Education, who is in charge of renewing annual digging permits, announced not long ago that "Those archaeologists who are not helpful to our effort to stop antiquities smuggling out of Turkey will no longer be able to excavate in our country."

Both Turkish officials and American archaeologists know, of course, that it isn't the archaeologists who are stealing. It is the old combination—already familiar from the stories of Greece and Italy, of Syria and Egypt—of the peasant farmer quite literally "moonlighting" in the tombs, the unscrupulous middleman, and the rich collector abroad, public or private, who covets a beautiful bit of the past. In their zeal to keep sticky fingers away from their treasures, Turkish officials have reached something of a triumph of bureaucratic muddle and idiotic secrecy.

On September 18, 1970, for example, the Turkish News Service carried the following story on the teleprinter that delivers its news to papers and other news-gathering agencies inside Turkey: "Villagers digging for a well in Ilgin, a town in the province of Konya, have uncovered a large Hittite monument which the Education Ministry's Orhan Oguz said 'may be one of the greatest archaeological finds in recent years.' The monument, made of stone blocks, was found two meters [just over 6 feet 6 inches] underground with hieroglyphics on it to the praise of the Hittite King Tuthalya IV, son of Hattusil III. Ministry sources say the monument is at least 3,250 years old. Writings on it, sources said, are the oldest found in Anatolia, five centuries earlier than all other known writings. The monument was decorated with royal arms and a Hittite sun symbol."

All very well, as far as it went. Instantly, of course, newspapers, aware of the enormous interest in new archaeological finds, began telephoning the Ministry of Education to find out more. One girl in an American news-gathering agency in Ankara made a record of her own telephone call to the Ministry. It reads like dialogue out of the book *Catch-22*:

GIRL: Hello, I'm calling to find out about the new Hittite find.

MINISTRY SPOKESMAN: What new Hittite find?

GIRL: The one the Minister of Education, Mr. Orguz, made the announcement about.

M.S.: Did the Minister make an announcement?

GIRL: Yes, he said this may be the most important Hittite find ever. We'd just like to know if digging is still going on, and who's digging, how long it will take to excavate the monument, and so forth.

M.S.: Well, there's not much I can tell you. There is no dig yet. Our Minister will announce more about it when he sees fit.

GIRL: But how can it be possible that tablets with pictures and writing were found, if there is no digging going on?

M.S.: One can't find out about a monumental discovery of this sort without patience.

GIRL: We are willing to be patient. But we would just like some advice, some guidance, as to when there might be more details. Perhaps we could be allowed to see the site, to take photographs and follow the developments there . . .

M.S.: We're still getting organized over all this, you must understand.

GIRL: Of course I understand. But when do you think you'll start digging?

M.S.: We are digging.

GIRL: Oh, right now? Who is digging?

M.S.: We cannot say that right now.

End of conversation.

8

THE TREASURE OF TROY

One of the great romances of all archaeology is the discovery of the ancient city of Troy, on the western shore of modern Turkey, by an amateur named Heinrich Schliemann who used the poet Homer as a road map. Schliemann was wrong in almost all his assessments, and he was destructive in his methods. The treasure he found, hid, and smuggled away vanished again twenty-five years ago and hasn't been seen in public since. Yet Schliemann found Troy.

Fabled Troy was hardly ever more than a village, by today's measurements, but it and the Trojan War loom larger in the minds and hearts—and histrionics—of the world's intellectuals than many another, larger city and more important war. Some people sing opera in the bathroom; others declaim Homeric details of the Trojan war at small gatherings of like-minded friends. Even nonintellectuals say casually "to work like a Trojan," paying unconscious tribute to the efforts of the citizens of Troy to hold out against invading Greeks of more than three thousand years ago. And everyone knows, vaguely, about Achilles and his vulnerable heel, about the beautiful Helen who "launched a thousand ships," about the wooden "Trojan horse," out of which crept Greek soldiers to unlock the gates of the city and bring about its fall.

Homer created all that fame—Homer the blind poet. He wrote so soaringly about the gods and goddesses, the heroes and the villains of a ten-year war that may or may not really have taken place, that one hundred generations of men and women have all but memorized his words. Homer's *Iliad* and *Odyssey* for centuries were revered on a plane with the Bible.

If the Hittites had had a Homer, then the town of Hattusas would today be as famous as Troy, or Athens, or Rome, or Jerusalem.

The Trojan War was so real to the ancients that it is fair to say that history began with it. Its dates, generally considered to have been 1194–1184 B.C., may or may not be correct. But its fame was such, and its gods believed to be so powerful, that all the travelers and the rulers of the ancient world went out of their way to visit it. Xerxes, the King of Persia and of most of the world in his time (about 519–465 B.C.), stopped there on his way to invade Greece and climbed up to its ancient citadel to sacrifice a thousand oxen to the Trojan goddess Athena. Alexander the Great (356–323 B.C.) headed back that way (but going in the other direction) to invade Persia. He too made a ritual stop at Troy, and, so the story goes, he ran, oiled and naked, around the tomb of Achilles and announced grand plans to rebuild the city. Julius Caesar (about 100–44 B.C.) paused there on his way to Egypt and found nothing but burned and ruined stones and an enveloping thicket of forest and scrub. Yet in this place, a city even then half of legend and half of fact, the great Caesar stepped on a patch of grass and believed it when someone shouted at him, "This is where they brought Hector's body. Don't offend his ghost!"

As the slow centuries passed and the pagan gods fell one by one before the rise of Judaism, Christianity, and Islam, Troy ceased to be a place of pilgrimage. It even ceased to be a city. Its site was forgotten, and there were many who said it had never existed. There were even, as we have noted earlier, scholars who said that Homer himself never existed, that the great books were compendiums of ancient writings put together and edited by unknown hands. Troy existed, for these people, only as a mythical city inhabited by mythical persons in books written by a mythical author.

It was Heinrich Schliemann who put Troy back on the maps and in the process put himself into the history books. Schliemann was born in 1822 in a small German town near the border of Poland, the son of a poor but emphatically not proper Protestant clergyman. On the Christmas when his son was seven, the clergyman gave him a book called *Illustrated History of the World.* Young Heinrich's eyes fell upon an illustration of Troy in flames. In the foreground was Aeneas, the heroic Trojan who survived the war and who by some accounts was the founder of the city of Rome. Aeneas in the drawing was trudging along stolidly, carrying his father on his back and holding his young son by the hand. They were fleeing the burning city, and yet they didn't seem to be either afraid or in any particular hurry. In the background, visible through the flames, were massive masonry walls. Young Heinrich fell in love with that picture, and he never forgot it.

Who doesn't have such a picture embedded forever in that dim gray area which was childish confusion between fact and fancy, the wonderful days of the discovery of the world? For every child discovers the world, including Troy, and his own village, and the nearest river, and all the rest. I remember a picture in a fifth-grade history book which purported to be Magellan Discovering the Pacific. He was standing on a sort of rock and parting some tall weeds with his hands. I remember thinking that the weeds looked like the cattails which grew by our local river, and which could be soaked in kerosene and set alight as torches, parents permitting. In my memory, Magellan bears a look of permanent surprise, as if he hadn't known that the Pacific was right out there behind those cattails. I shivered with Magellan at the sense of discovery, and I was as thunderstruck by it all as he appeared to be. Not until many years later did it dawn on me that he didn't exactly "discover" the Pacific: millions of people who lived in it and around it must have noticed that it was there, long before he did.

But that is quibbling. What Magellan was for me so must Aeneas and the flames of Troy have been for young Heinrich. It was to be forty years before he saw the ruins of the city for himself, but he lived with the drawing and its message all that time. When he was ten, his Christmas present to his father was a dissertation on Troy, written in Latin.

When Heinrich was about fourteen the family's finances collapsed, and the young man was taken out of school and sent to a menial job in a grocer's shop. It was an existence Dickensian in its discomfort. Heinrich slept on the floor, rose at 5 A.M. to sweep out, and spent eighteen hours a day wrestling kegs of herring and bottles of potato whiskey out of the basement for the customers in the shop.

In later years Schliemann remembered only one beautiful episode: the time a drunken miller lurched into the store, in search no doubt of potato whiskey. While Heinrich went to fetch it, the miller suddenly began reciting something sonorous, at the top of his lungs. It was Greek, and it was Homer on Troy. Heinrich didn't speak Greek, but he liked the sound, and he adored hearing of his favorite city. (In Greek the city was called Ilion, in Latin Ilium, after Ilus, its legendary founder; English-speaking people call it Troy after Ilus' father, Tros, who had given that name to the country.) So carried away was Heinrich that he dug a few pennies out of the pallet he slept on and spent them paying for more whiskey to persuade the miller to recite some more. Heinrich didn't know it at the time, but all he got for his pennies was the same one hundred lines of the *Iliad* over and over again. The miller had learned them as a youth, just before he was flung out of school for some now-forgotten misdemeanor. They were the only words in Greek he knew, but he must have recited them well, because they so inspired Heinrich Schliemann that he threw over his job in the grocery store and went off to Hamburg to seek his fortune.

The phrase sounds old-fashioned nowadays, but in Schliemann's time young men *did* "seek their fortune," though few found quite so many fortunes as Heinrich. His new life started out very badly, however. Somehow he managed to sign onto a freighter headed for Venezuela, but he began the voyage too seasick to move and he ended it shipwrecked off the coast of Holland. Some friendly Dutchman fished him half-frozen out of the water and helped him find a job as a messenger boy for a company of international traders. Heinrich spoke only German, but he quickly learned Dutch, English, French, Spanish, Italian, and Portuguese, and when an opportunity came for a job in Czarist Russia, he learned Russian. He made his first million or so as an international trader in indigo, a blue dye much prized in his era. Then he went off to California ostensibly to see about the personal affairs of a brother, and made another fortune during the gold rush. He made still a third by wheeling and dealing during the Crimean War, and in his spare time between making and counting his money he rather casually learned Polish, Swedish, and—at last—Greek.

In later years he explained this curious delay in learning Greek. He loved Homer so much, he said, that he was afraid if he ever learned Greek he would fall completely under the spell of the language and the land and he would rush off to Greece forever, abandoning the world of commerce.

That is in fact exactly what happened to him, in 1868—but a man with three fortunes should be able to abandon commerce at last. His first marriage, to a chilly Russian aristocrat, had been a disaster, and now that he had decided to yield to his passion for Greece, the rather odd Mr. Schliemann decided also to yield to a Greek bride. He wrote friends asking that they send him photographs of suitable young ladies, and in due course he married one named Sophie, who made him happy for the rest of his life.

He hadn't actually decided to become an archaeologist on that first trip in 1868, but after a brief stop on the island of Ithaca he made straight for the Turkish mainland to look for the site of Troy. By 1868, most people who still believed that Troy had been a real city had decided that it must have been located beneath or near the little Turkish village of Bunarbashi. Just why they had come to this decision is not quite clear, but it was toward Bunarbashi that Schliemann set out, with a guide and two horses provided by the Russian consul in Constantinople. Bunarbashi stood then, as now, on the great flat "plain of Troy" beside the straits of the Dardanelles which separate Europe from Asia. The Mt. Ida of which Homer wrote is visible from Bunarbashi, and it seemed to Schliemann that the little town was in the right general area. There was one enormous defect, however: Homer said quite clearly that the invading Greeks were able to make seven or eight journeys a day from their moored invasion ships to the walls of the beleaguered Troy. Yet Bunarbashi was a good 10 miles from the sea. Not even an Olympic runner could make 140 or 160 miles a day. Had Bunarbashi been near the sea in 1194 B.C.? Many an ancient site in Turkey has "retreated from the sea" in the process of the silting of its rivers and swamps in the ensuing centuries.

Schliemann decided to look for other clues. Homer had written also of two "fair-flowing springs, where two fountains rise that feed deep-eddying Skamandros," the river. Energetically, Schliemann hired a local guide and set out to hunt for the two springs. To his dismay, in one day they found not only two springs but thirty-four. Later the guide dashed Schliemann even more by pointing out that they had missed a few. There really were forty springs near Bunarbashi, he said, which accounted for the local name of the region, "the forty eyes."

Clutching his dog-eared copy of Homer, the relentless Schliemann made one final test. There was a quite famous account of how Achilles "the brave runner" had chased the hero Hector three times around the walls of Troy while all those interfering gods and goddesses sat back and watched and chose up sides. Schliemann decided to take a stroll around the Bunarbashi mound that purported to be the ruins of Troy, to decide whether or not Achilles and Hector could have done it three times at full tilt. Most of the way around the mound was easy enough, but at one point there was a clifflike bank so steep that Schliemann had to go down it backward, almost on hands and knees. Wouldn't Homer have mentioned this obstacle in the path of his brave runners "in hasty flight"? This actually wasn't a very good point, because in three thousand years many a sudden drop could have been created by digging, and many a local landmark altered beyond description.

Even more damaging to the Bunarbashi theory was the absence of massive walls anywhere near it. Schliemann couldn't forget the walls that had been visible through the flames in his childhood picture. The artist had imagined it all, of course, but other cities of the age of Troy still had remnants of walls. Not entirely reluctantly, Schliemann abandoned the search at Bunarbashi. The town was a miserable place of mosquitoes, dung heaps, poverty, and bad smells, and he decided to go look somewhere else.

There were mounds and bits of ruin strewn all over the plain of Troy, but Schliemann was attracted particularly to a mound at the Turkish village called Hissarlik. It lay to the north of Bunarbashi and was much nearer to the sea. From the top of the mound one could see the blue water glinting in the distance, less than one hour's walk away, and to the viewer standing there Mt. Ida was over his left shoulder. Hissarlik's mound was disturbingly small, less than 100 feet above the plain and little larger than a football field. Could such a small place have held out for ten years, and could it have accommodated all those gods and goddesses, all those heroes, the beautiful Helen, *and* the wooden horse? It seemed unlikely, although the mound was gently sloping and its perimeter had no sudden drops or precipices. It was possible that Achilles and Hector, in the heat of battle, could have made it around the perimeter walls three times even brandishing their battle weapons and sweating inside their armor.

Before he started to dig, Schliemann went off to Constantinople to talk with knowledgeable foreigners there. Among the men he consulted was a remarkable Englishman who in those somewhat more casual days served as vice-consul for the Americans. His name was Frank Calvert, and he was convinced that Hissarlik's mound was the site of Troy. He was so convinced, in fact, that he had actually bought half the mound some years before in order to dig on it. He had made some trenches and found the remains of an ancient structure made with huge blocks of worked stone. Calvert had written an account of his find for the *Archaeological Journal* and tried hard but unsuccessfully to get the British to conduct a full-scale excavation. Now, partly perhaps because he was annoyed with the British for ignoring his advice, Calvert offered to help Schliemann. Generously, he gave permission to this strange, arrogant man to dig on his half of the mound. Calvert didn't ask a thing for himself, and he even offered the advice that a long-term resident of Turkey could provide to a brash newcomer. Schliemann couldn't dig at all without a *firman*, or permit, from the Turkish government, Calvert explained, and besides, it was too late in the season to begin. Nevertheless, he let Schliemann tramp all over his mound, measure its dimensions, and dream his dreams of Achilles and Hector. Calvert even explained the nagging problem of the "two fair-flowing springs." This particular part of old Anatolia was a volcanic region in which hot springs suddenly appeared, dried up, and then as suddenly reappeared. Springs, like the oracles of the ancient world, can be sometime things.

Almost two years passed before Schliemann got permission to dig, and all that time he bombarded the long-suffering Calvert with questions about his upcoming excavations. "When is the best time to begin work? Do I have to take a tent and iron bedstead and pillow with me? How much time will it take to dig away the artificial mountain? What sort of hat is best against the scorching sun?"

In a display of patience that would have been the envy of Homer's Penelope herself, Calvert replied to all the questions and helped pull strings with the government; and finally, in 1870, Schliemann descended like a fury upon the mound at Hissarlik. He arrived proudly with his youthful Greek bride, Sophie, and so enamored was he of both Sophie and the Greek world that he insisted upon bestowing Homeric names upon his little band of workmen. A Turkish peasant who had been called Nasredding or Timur all his life suddenly discovered that the boss was calling him Bellerophon, or Telamon, or Calches. It was a bit confusing, and so was Schliemann's habit of supervising the work with a whip in his hand and a pistol in his belt. He had made the peasants heroes of the Homeric world by name, but in the deplorable modern age of 1870 he feared their recalcitrance or perhaps dishonesty. There is no indication that he ever used either the whip or the pistol, but he kept them handy.

Though his friend Calvert owned the eastern half of the Hissarlik mound and had given permission to dig there, Schliemann characteristically decided to dig on the western half, which overlooked the sea. This half belonged to a pair of Turks whom Schliemann had never laid eyes on, but he was not bothered by this. He started with ten workmen with shovels, and after the first hour's digging they had found the remnants of a wall. In one day in the blazing heat, the renamed Bellerophon, Telamon, and their mates had uncovered foundations 60 feet long and 40 feet wide. After the third day they had found some flagstones of a floor, the remains of ancient sheep dung, and clear evidence of a disastrous fire.

Then something very odd happened to Schliemann. Perhaps he reverted to his previous nature as a fortune-making businessman. Whatever it was, he suddenly abandoned his scholarly approach to Troy and turned into a treasure hunter. The audacious dreamer who had started out to prove that Homer was a good reporter as well as a magnificent poet became a man with the frenzy for gold in his heart. He ordered his diggers to start hacking out deep trenches to crisscross the mound. Dutifully the men went to work, battering down any masonry walls that impeded their progress. "Trenching" is a quite legitimate quick way to assess the value of a mysterious mound—but progress should be carefully noted and charted, and records kept. Schliemann didn't bother, and he was caught in his destructive act by the two Turkish owners of that half of the mound.

It must have been quite an encounter, between the sputtering Turks who found a small army of trespassing diggers swarming over their hillside and the arrogant Schliemann, who refused to stop. For some reason this master linguist had never bothered to learn Turkish, and he tried to explain through an interpreter that he was doing work of a highly important scientific nature. The Turks were unimpressed. Then their eyes hit upon the huge blocks of stone that Schliemann's diggers had exposed. They announced that they had long intended to build a bridge over a nearby river, and these old stones would do the job very well. In an ominous foretaste of what was to come in Turkey, Schliemann agreed, and the Turks started hauling away the stone for their bridge. Within weeks they were back, saying that they had enough stone and that Schliemann must cease and desist upon their land. There was nothing to do but leave, which Schliemann did, but the enduring damage to the ruins and to serious archaeology had already been done.

For two more years Schliemann carried on a running, sneaking battle with the Turkish government over his Homer-bestowed right to dig for Troy. Each year he hacked away a little more. He found cyclopean walls, jars as tall as a man, and two gates 20 feet apart that might have been grand enough for Troy. He found coins, lance heads, boars' teeth, little glistening black phallic symbols (*phalloi*), and to his dismay he found dozens of little clay objects shaped like owls. The owls baffled him, and he went back to his floppy copy of Homer to find an explanation. Homer had called the goddess Pallas Athena "owl-faced"; maybe that was the answer. Then he came upon objects that looked like spinning tops with two holes bored into them. Would the Trojan King Priam have passed his days with spinning tops and clay owls? Schliemann was depressed and worried. Surely he and Homer couldn't both have been wrong. Had he found Troy, or had he found some prehistoric village dedicated to the worship of spinning tops, owls, and phallic symbols? It was the owls that bothered him most, and at night in the excavation real live owls came out to taunt him and to trouble his sleep. On the night of March 15, 1873, he wrote in his journal that "The misery of life in this wilderness is increased by the innumerable owls who build their nests in the holes in the walls I have excavated. There is something mysterious and horrible in their screeching; it is unbearable . . ."

Perhaps it is true that "it is always darkest before the dawn." Within days after that gloomy entry in his diary, Schliemann found the Treasure of Troy. The world will never know for sure just when he found it, because he never revealed the details. But it was in the spring of 1873, and the discovery created a sensation that was not to be duplicated for almost fifty years: not until 1922, when British archaeologists uncovered the treasure of "King Tut's tomb" in Egypt.

Schliemann's treasure came to light just as he was about to conclude his dig. The buttercups of early spring had turned brown, the howling heat of Turkey was pressing hard on the diggers, and the amateur archaeologist had already announced he was leaving the field to retire to Athens and write a book. To make the best use of his few remaining days of work, Schliemann had hired 160 diggers and set them to work in small groups all over the mound.

He trotted back and forth peering down one hole and then another. Suddenly, at about 7 A.M., he peered into a dig near one of the great gates in a city wall, and 28 feet down he saw a copper box with a strange design. The box looked about 3 feet long and 18 inches high, and there were two helmet-shaped objects on its lid. Schliemann decided instantly that whatever was in that box would be treasure, and it would be his. His young wife, Sophie, was standing near him, and the Turkish government representative who was there to keep an eye on the dig was for the moment nowhere in sight. Schliemann thought fast.

"Sophie, my dear," he said quietly, "you must go at once and shout to all the workmen, *Paidos*' [rest period]." Sophie was thunderstruck. "A rest period so early, at seven in the morning?" she asked. Her disbelief was understandable: Schliemann had spent half his time trying to coax more work from his diggers, the other half of his time complaining bitterly about the number of religious holidays available to Greek and Turkish workmen. Now, suddenly, he seemed to want to give them a day off.

"Tell them that I've just remembered that it's my birthday," he said. "Tell them I'll pay full wages for the day, but that they may return to their villages. Hurry, and shout, *Paidos.*'"

Sophie, like most mere humans within the orbit of Heinrich Schliemann, did as she was told. She climbed the ladder up out of the excavation trench, delivered her husband's strange message, then climbed back down again. After all that effort, she was sent back up the ladder to "Go get your big shawl, your big red shawl." While she was dutifully performing this errand, Sophie noticed that the workmen had vanished. She came back with the shawl and found her husband hacking away with a pocketknife at the dirt and stone that surrounded the copper container. The fortification wall, weakened by the trench, was shifting and settling and threatening to fall on his head, but Schliemann just kept hacking away. Finally he got the container free and opened its lid, and there was the treasure: 56 golden earrings, 8,750 gold rings and buttons, silver knife blades, copper daggers and lance heads, silver goblets, two golden diadems (small crownlike ornaments shaped like a headband). Nothing like these diadems had ever been seen before; one was made of ninety separate chains of gold with leaf and flower pendants hanging down.

The census above was not taken right that minute, down in the trench. Schliemann counted later, after he had bundled the whole thing into Sophie's red shawl and scuttled back with it to the little wooden expedition house. In a moment of gay abandon back there, he even wrapped the diadems around the faithful Sophie's forehead and decked her fingers with rings. He was beside himself. He was sure he had found King Priam's treasure from Troy (he hadn't, actually), and no force on earth would now take it away from him. On May 30, 1873, he sent a strange letter to his friend Frank Calvert's brother Frederick. By a strange irony, Frederick Calvert owned 5,000 acres of land near Bunarbashi, the first place Schliemann had searched for Troy, and now in his letter Schliemann informed Frederick Calvert that he was taking the liberty of depositing at Bunarbashi "six baskets and a bag" for temporary safekeeping. Under no circumstances, Schliemann told Frederick Calvert, should any Turk get his hands on them. In the harmless-looking six baskets and a bag was, of course, the Treasure of Troy.

Instantly rumors started, from whatever age-old fount rumors come from, and the Turkish watchman/supervisor on the Hissarlik dig turned up at the expedition house to ask Schliemann what was happening and what he had found. Schliemann threw him out, almost bodily. Even as he did so, the treasure was being smuggled out of Turkey by means still unknown but along routes that are doubtless still used today. Apparently most of the treasure went in small, anonymous straw-wrapped parcels delivered to Schliemann's Greek in-laws near Athens. Late at night they were buried discreetly inside faceless farmyards, behind stables, near barns.

In an astonishing display of restraint, Schliemann himself stayed on at Troy for a few more weeks, and it is said that before he left he had the excavation site blessed by a priest. There can't have been much left to bless: the whole mound looked like a gigantic mole-infested garden, or a target site after saturation bombing. Schliemann announced, dramatically, that he was leaving Troy forever.

He did return, of course, more than once, but the next few years were completely dominated by his strenuous efforts to keep the treasure for himself. He wrote pseudoscientific articles for every publication he could find, touting the treasure of the Trojan King Priam as one of the greatest finds of all history. Later on, the world was to hear a lot about "the curse of the Pharaohs," a mysterious curse that apparently caused bad luck to anyone who touched the tomb of a Pharaoh in Egypt. All that was fifty years away from Heinrich Schliemann and the Treasure of Troy; but in retrospect, it seems that Schliemann too had a curse. The moment he began bragging about what he had found, he was embroiled in international protests and demands. The Turks, quite reasonably, rushed first into the fray to demand that he return the treasure he had smuggled out of their country. He ignored them completely, though he did have the decency to try to defend the Turkish watchman whom he had so carefully hoodwinked. This man's name was Amin, and the Turks were threatening to punish him. Punishment in those days was quite often fatal, so Schliemann wrote a letter saying that "I found the treasure while Amin Effendi was working on another part of the mound altogether. If you had seen the despair written on the poor man's face when he learned about it . . . you would have pity on him." He didn't bother to add that he had thrown Amin out of the house when he came to check on the treasure.

Turkey wasn't the only nation that wanted the treasure. There was Greece, which felt it had some vested interest in the Trojan War. There was England, with its great museums, eager to buy. There was Russia, where, after all, Schliemann had made his first fortune, found his first wife, had his first family. There was Germany, the country of his birth.

Schliemann ignored them all. Spraying the world with alternate compliments and insults, he calmly built a palatial home in Athens to house his treasure. He called his house Iliou Melathron ("the palace of Troy"), and shamelessly he displayed in it the goblets and diadems, the lance heads and rings. Throughout his gaudy life, he insisted that messages be sent to him in classical Greek. He named the two children of his second marriage Andromache and Agamemnon, and some say that to the end of his life he wore in his suit-coat pocket a bright red handkerchief in memory of Sophie's red shawl in which he had carried away the treasure of Troy.

What, exactly, did Schliemann find? Later, more skillful archaeologists are convinced that he dug up not the Homeric Trojan treasure at all but a much earlier, probably late–Bronze Age hoard of an unknown king. Much of it was primitive, much of it wasn't truly gold, but it was more valuable than gold because of its great age. Unfortunately, all of it now has vanished. Toward the end of his life Schliemann exhibited his treasure, to great excitement, in London, and then he gave it as a present to Berlin. In 1945, victorious soldiers of the Soviet Union took it away from Berlin, and it has never been seen since.

Yet he did find Troy, one of the Troys. It is clear now that ancient structures on this site went through nine major periods, each broken into subperiods or subepochs. Modern archaeologists believe that Schliemann was at about Level II (2400–2200 B.C. or earlier), whereas the Troy of Homer must be at the top of Level VI and the beginning of Level VII.

Around the ravaged hillside by the sea the arguments still rage. Some believe it was a small city; others say it never was a city at all but only a fortress guarding a small natural height. Some skeptics cite the historian Herodotus (about 484–425 B.C.,) who wrote that the beautiful Helen wasn't anywhere near the place during the Trojan War. Now, Herodotus lived about seven hundred years after the war is supposed to have been fought, so he was much more distant from it than Homer, who lived only a century and a half after it. But Herodotus said he had interviewed some Egyptian priests about the famous conflict, and they told him that Helen had fled from Troy and taken refuge in Memphis, Egypt, because she was just plain fed up with the jealousy between her husband, Menelaus, and her lover, Paris. Menelaus himself, according to Herodotus, made the long voyage to Egypt to hunt for his wife and found her "none the worse for her adventure." If this is true, she was a very fortunate lady. Everyone else who got mixed up in the thing, including scholars who try to untangle its events, emerged wounded or worn out.

A distinguished modern Turkish archaeologist, Ekrem Akur-

These are some of the walls of "Homer's Troy," excavated and slightly rebuilt by archaeologists.

gal, has argued eloquently (*Ancient Civilizations and Ruins of Turkey*, 1969) that the broad outlines of Homer's Trojan War are correct, and that Troy did indeed exist, but that the details of the war were quite different from the Homeric version. From clear evidence of a disastrous earthquake and a fire that destroyed Level VI, and from subtle but notable differences in architectural style that came with Level VII, Akurgal reconstructs the events as follows:

Achaean Greeks, pushing relentlessly eastward in their drive for new lands and new settlements, crashed head on into an indigenous people in the fortress of Troy, at about the same period in history described by Homer. The site of Troy, on a small height overlooking a fertile plain and the straits of the Dardanelles, was a perfect defense spot. Then as now, the straits were the dividing point between Europe and Asia, and in that era before bridges and thoroughfares were built, whoever held Troy could command the point at which invaders from both directions would be forced to pass.

Thus, Akurgal says, the Achaeans came to Troy about 1194 B.C. and they fought for ten years. But Troy fell, according to him, not because of the heroism of the Greeks or even because of the intervention of the gods, but because the earthquake knocked down the walls and admitted the invading Greeks. The *Iliad*, he says, could be an account of the unsuccessful attempt of the Achaean Greeks to capture the Troy of Level VI. When the *Odyssey* begins, we are told the Achaeans took Troy through the ruse of the Trojan Horse. Akurgal believes the horse came later. Troy VI was destroyed, and the invading Greeks entered the ruined city. Then they rebuilt it in the different style of Troy VII, but it was still "Homeric" because Homer spoke of the eventual triumph of the Greeks.

According to his theory, Akurgal explains, "The stratagem of the wooden horse takes a meaning. The Achaeans, unable to capture the city of Ilion [Troy] after fighting for 10 years, could only achieve their object after the city had been destroyed. . . . Since the Achaeans knew well that they owed their victory to Poseidon, the Earth-Shaker, they offered up a wooden statue in the shape of [a] horse in memory of their gratitude. . . ."

Nowadays many a visitor to Turkey is told, "Don't go to Troy. It's nothing but a hole in the ground."

This is not true. The approach to it from the south is exciting, along a smooth road which rises slowly up from the heat of the plains into cool air and hairpin highway turns, with pine trees bordering the road. The "mound of Hissarlik" doesn't look much like a mound any more, because, as Seton Lloyd said, to excavate a mound is to destroy it. There are on the site a small museum, a parking lot, and a row of ramshackle souvenir stands named, in-

From this vantage point, the Trojans could have seen the Greek ships coming into the harbor just beyond the plain of Troy.

evitably I suppose, things like "Helen and Paris" and "The Wooden Horse."

Then there is Troy. One climbs a few stone steps, modern, and suddenly there is the pedestal of a Greek column, upside down, with a stark sign behind it which says, "Troya, Troy." Behind that, tumbled rock, light, air, the plain of Troy, and the glittering sea. One small neat sign says, "Wall, Troy VII," and the visitor must read his guidebook to discover that this is Homeric Troy.

There are walls of all its eras, the remnants of Roman theaters, and an ancient gate and ramp. There are blurred inscriptions, and lichen-covered old scrollwork in stone, but there is very little that summons up Achilles and Hector, Helen and the horse. For me, the visit to Troy was saved by a nice young Italian and his American bride. The Italian was showing off, as Italians will, translating a French guidebook first into Italian and then into English for his bride. He led her up to a pinnacle on the ancient walls and he waved his skinny right arm and he said, "There— right there—they fought. There on the plain of Troy. And there was the harbor for the thousand ships of Greece. Over there is Mount Ida. And here, here where we stand, here is where the Trojans stood."

Then he cleared his throat and he recited Homer, from memory, in Latin. Suddenly as his young voice rolled on, even I could see the ships, hear the shouts. Blind Homer had saved his city one more time.

9

ROOFTOPS FULL OF DOORS

Of all the "holes in the ground" that archaeologists have strewn across ancient Anatolia, none is more deceptive than the site of Çatal Hüyük. It is a dust-colored series of holes, surrounded by a straggling wire fence and guarded by a little man with a uniform cap. He has a rifle, but he usually leaves it in his sleeping shack down by the gate.

Once there were forests across this rugged land, woods full of leopards, stags, and giant cattle. "We once discovered a wild-bull horn six feet long," says archaeologist James Mellaart, who found and excavated the ancient city. "Add two of these horns together, and put a head in between, and you have a giant. No wonder they painted giants on their walls."

Today the forests are gone, and the giant cattle too. There are storks in the landscape, and layer after layer of dust. There is the thin line of an irrigation canal with hand-operated wells at intervals, their long counterbalanced wooden poles each suspending a black leather bucket from the end. At a distance they look like huge one-legged birds against the hot blue sky.

When you gaze at the molehill that is today's Çatal Hüyük, it is difficult indeed to comprehend that this "city" is one of the most

The site of Çatal Hüyük, one of the most exciting archaeological finds ever made. For political reasons, digging has been abandoned since the season of 1965, and although bits of brick wall are still visible, wind and rain are gradually turning the whole area into a mudhole.

exciting ever discovered. It was six times as big as Troy and five thousand years older. As its wonders came out of the ground, they rewrote the history of mankind and upset all the careful statistical charts that tried to show when man became a city dweller, and when he invented pottery, and when he began to domesticate animals.

The guard of Çatal Hüyük is also a guide, and he delivers his speech so softly one has to strain to hear him: "Here, we have taken six habitation levels from the top, and there are six more beneath it. The city covered thirty-two acres and probably held three thousand people at a time. It was at its peak from about 6500 before Christ to 5600 before Christ."

Such age staggers the imagination: a city almost nine thousand years old. Then there is a deeper hole in the ground, and the guide points. "See the two fireplaces, one about three feet above the other? Two totally different habitation levels, one on top of the other. See the black streak, through the rock? Fire. Fire destroyed one settlement after another, and they built again on top."

Rain, wind, time have totally erased remnants of the red, white and black wall murals of Çatal Hüyük which are believed to be mankind's first proper murals, the artistic descendants of cave paintings. Çatal Hüyük is neolithic in age (a period of time roughly 7000–5600 B.C. in most of the Middle East) —one of the cities that marked the great revolution when men moved out of caves and into towns. Fortunately, the best of the murals were removed at the time of excavation, and they are handsomely displayed today in the Ankara Archaeological Museum together with a reconstruction of the rooms where these people lived: rooms decorated with series of bulls' horns, with little clay figurines of the pregnant mother goddess, with raised platforms under which they buried their ancestors, once the vultures had picked their bones clean.

On the day I visited the site, the guard was so lonely that he invited me back to his sleeping shack for afternoon tea. Carefully he unlocked the wooden door and led me into a room about 10 feet by 6 feet. The plank walls were covered with color photographs of Turkey, torn from magazines and pinned against strips of oilcloth. He had a bed, a tiny stove, a teapot, and the trusty rifle leaning in a corner. He waved his arm around this little domain and made an archaeologist's joke: "My neolithic house, Level One."

Then he walked me to the car, and on the way I suddenly stopped to pick up what appeared to be a terra-cotta (reddish baked clay) jar handle. I turned it over in my hand, then showed it to the guard, and he sniffed. "Nothing," he said. "That's Roman." He scuffed about a bit in the dust, leaned over, and picked up a tiny bit of black pottery. "This," he said, "is neolithic. About eight thousand years old." Then he spotted a tiny fragment of what looked like black glass, shaped like a thin triangle, and he put it into my hand. "Obsidian," he said. "It made

The guard at Çatal Hüyük stands (left) outside what he calls his "neolithic house, Level One" with his son and two friends.

their fortune in Çatal Hüyük. They made mirrors of it, and they shaved with it. Obsidian was better than gold when this city was great."

Obsidian is volcanic glass formed naturally by the heat and minerals in volcanoes, and the ancient town of Çatal Hüyük had a very rich source in the nearby mountain called Hasan Dagh, 10,000 feet high. Geologists say that the volcanic peaks which still surround Çatal Hüyük were active until four thousand years ago, so those faraway people were quite accustomed to seeing the mountains blow up.

One of the most fascinating wall paintings ever found may in fact be a painting of Hasan Dagh. Archaeologists found it in a shrine at Çatal Hüyük. It is 9 feet long, and it covered two walls of an ancient structure that once had a fine reed matting on the floor. The painting is crude but precise: across the lower foreground are what at first glance appear to be about eighty boxes— no two exactly alike, but each a little self-contained square connected to its neighbors. Off in the background is a strange object with two peaks or cones. This seems to be a mountain. There are bits spurting out of the right-hand top, and a cloud of dots and strokes going out from that. After a careful study, and an examination of the site of the city as it looks today, archaeologists believe that this is actually a neolithic rendition of the town, with the twin peaks of the volcano Hasan Dagh in eruption in the distance, hurling out glowing volcanic "bombs" and red-hot stones. It may well be the world's first landscape painting.

Volcanoes in eruption have always fascinated human beings. When Europe's tallest volcano, Etna in Sicily, erupted in the spring of 1971, so many thousands of tourists rushed to the area to watch that the Italian national police had to be called out to keep the curious from getting killed in the lava flow. As the great peaks rumble, split open, hurl molten rock into the air, some sort of primitive reaction overcomes even the most sophisticated of modern men. Well-educated Americans, Englishmen, Scandinavians actually applauded in the spring of 1971 as Etna's lava crept down the slopes, swallowing up vineyards and pine trees and gateposts in its advance. It devoured a steel bridge slowly, and millions sat transfixed before their television sets to watch as the steel beams writhed in the heat, melted, and collapsed.

What it must have been nine thousand years ago, eight thousand years ago, when the mountains blew up! If bulls had a horn span of 13 feet, what powerful gods must have lived in the fire of the mountains. Hasan Dagh itself must have been considered a god. But even more than that, the volcano was the source of obsidian, the very livelihood of the old city. Obsidian from this mountain was of a sharpness and a transparency unknown from other sources of the ancient world. Further, it was so fine it could reflect images perfectly. It may have been the first time that men and women could stare at their own reflections in a perfect surface. Surely they had seen their faces, their bodies, in the rippling reflections of pools and streams, but now, in the chunks of perfect black volcanic glass, the images were still and accurate, the undulation of moving water removed. It is tempting to wonder if vanity was born with obsidian . . . but it is certain that in the mud huts of Çatal Hüyük, man stared at his own reflection, and it must have made him think.

Beautiful obsidian mirrors have been found at all levels in the city, mostly in shrines. The diggers also found obsidian beads, razors, daggers, and sewing instruments. There were flint tools which came from miles away, and there was pottery, but obviously the residents of Çatal Hüyük considered pottery too much trouble. They customarily made dishes and pots from worked stone, and for dry storage they had a finely developed industry of wooden bowls and woven baskets. This, archaeologists point out, is perfectly natural: a people surrounded by forests use the material at hand—wood and its by-products.

How, and why, did the archaeologist James Mellaart come to Çatal Hüyük, and how did he know it was important?

The selection of a mound to dig in was, for years, a matter of chance and the obvious. The sites of such famous old cities as Jericho, Nineveh, and Ur were simple. The remains were conspicuous, and folk tradition had carried the memories of their great days right down to the nineteenth and twentieth centuries, when men first began to dig for information instead of for treasure. But nobody had ever heard of Çatal Hüyük. Its "mound" was, to be sure, about 60 feet high, but it was set in a landscape dotted with such mounds. There was nothing to distinguish it from its fellows.

Mellaart began, in the 1950s, by tramping across the central regions of Anatolia. He was then a man in his twenties, unmarried, and a wizard with languages. He had a $1,000 scholarship to study archaeology in the field, and he made it last two long years as he explored the wilder reaches of the ancient plateau. He carried a rucksack full of food, and he had his pockets full of stones to hurl at prowling and aggressive sheep dogs. He picked up a little Turkish, and he talked to the curious peasants who assembled to stare at this strange foreigner with the baggy pants and the khaki shirt. He never dug, in those days; he merely looked and took notes. He noted down carefully all the mounds he located, and he learned to know exactly where to look: at points where an ancient road crossed a river (as in Samsat, where Meezgole dug her mound), at the crossings of old trails, at natural defense points. He picked up bits of pottery and sherds lying on the surface, to get a rough idea of the date of the top level of the mound. In the middle '50s he went to work with the British Institute of Archaeology in Turkey, and together with the dig director, Seton Lloyd, he helped excavate the Bronze Age city of Beycesultan.

Among archaeologists, James Mellaart has always had a reputation for being lucky. One day in Jericho he rose at dawn to go for a walk and noted a strange shadow on the earth; he walked over to investigate it and saw that it was, in fact, a slight depression. In any other light he wouldn't have noticed, but the low sun of early morning had thrown it into relief. He dug there, and he found forty intact ancient vases before breakfast. Another time, in Cyprus, he was helping a dig and refused an invitation to the nearest town because he didn't have any money for either the trip or the inevitable entertainment in town. All his companions went off, and the lonely Mellaart trudged back out to the dig—and turned up a treasure in Mycenean bronze. This famous "luck" was still with him in 1957 in Turkey. From gossip in a Turkish coffee shop he heard hints that a peasant had found something on his land near the town of Burdur. Mellaart went off to have a look, and found that enterprising villagers had been hacking away at a very small mound in the area and turning up brightly painted late chalcolithic (the Age of Copper) pottery dating from 3500–3000 B.C. Mellaart got permission to dig properly, and very soon he found the source of the pottery: a tiny prehistoric village of mud and brick surrounded by a mud enclosure wall. As he extended his dig, he found an even earlier village on the same site, which was bigger and far more elaborate. This always comes as a surprise to amateurs, but archaeologists know that sometimes very advanced civilizations are destroyed and followed by more primitive ones. Mellaart's "new," more deeply buried town appeared to be neolithic and thus thousands of years older than the chalcolithic one. This was the site of Hacilar, where even today the canny peasants are digging illegally and have actually turned to forging antiquities which have fooled some of the great museums. Once Hacilar was found, it was clear that civilization on the Anatolian plain was far older than had ever been proved before. Mellaart remembered that, years before, he had made a careful entry in his notebook: there was a mound in the Konya plain that he felt sure was "early neolithic" and quite huge for its period. If Hacilar was neolithic at the bottom, then certainly that great mound south of Konya was neolithic. In 1961 he began to dig at Çatal Hüyük.

A most astonishing picture emerged of the life there. The houses of these ancient people sometimes had walls 5 feet thick around the outer edge, and they were locked together side by side to form a fortification against the outside world. Construction was of simple mud, but with wooden beams and supports suggestive of the famous "half-timbered" houses of Great Britain in a much later age, and even of the typical two-story construction of many modern Turkish village houses, with the upper floor corbeled out to give greater floor space upstairs and provide shade for a porch downstairs. The flat-roofed houses of Çatal Hüyük had no doors at all, and tiny windows up under the eaves. Entrance obviously was from the roof, probably by means of wooden ladders. When a citizen of this old town wanted to go call on his neighbors, he had to walk over the rooftops and down the neighbors' ladder. The entire city was a defensive fortification, turning bare, inhospitable blank walls to the outside world. Inside, connected to little clusters of four or five houses, were shrines for the worship of the bull and the Great Mother, both obviously fertility symbols for the community.

Çatal Hüyük residents, like people today, built houses according to their private means—some large, some small. The basic form was always the same, however, the minimum being a single room with two raised platforms, a hearth, an oven, and a wooden ladder for getting in and out. The platforms probably served as beds, couches, tables. Each room, no matter how small, had two of them, and archaeologists believe that the smaller platform was the man's bed at night, the larger one being the province of his wife and children. The dead were buried inside the house, under the platforms, and the rite and cult of the dead is a fascinating story in Çatal Hüyük.

Mellaart and his men found well-preserved skeletons of men, women, and children under the platforms of some houses and many shrines. Most of the skeletons lay on the left side, with the head facing the inside of the house, the legs toward the wall. Some houses had as few as eight bodies, others as many as twenty-seven or thirty-two, depending, apparently, upon the number of generations each family stayed in the same house. There was a great preponderance of skeletons of women and children, because many males must have died far from home, on hunting expeditions or in wars or while out on trading parties. Most of the bones still formed intact skeletons, in a state of flexed limbs, with here and there desiccated sinews still holding the bones together. From a great deal of external evidence, including the presence of textiles and mats within the tombs, archaeologists believe that the flesh had been removed from the bodies before they were buried. Otherwise the decomposition of the body itself would have destroyed any woven materials or mats put in the tomb with it.

Wall paintings from two shrines give a macabre but very specific idea of just how the people of Çatal Hüyük dealt with their dead. The biggest of the paintings, 6 feet high, shows seven vultures, three flying to the right and four to the left, swooping down over six human corpses which are lying on their left sides, the traditional posture of the dead in the tombs. All six bodies are shown headless. This must have been the symbol for death, for in the tombs skulls were found with the bodies and, as archaeologist Mellaart pointed out in one of his reports, "vultures do not remove heads." The bodies of the dead must have been exposed for the vultures to pick clean; then the bones were gathered up and wrapped in cloth or placed in straw baskets to be "buried" under the platforms of the houses. The system was clean, extremely hygienic, and most efficient.

But still there are mysteries. . . . Many of the skulls, primarily those of the women, were painted with red ochre. In some cases the bones of the torso were also painted. Perhaps this was part of a general cult of ancestor worship, but archaeologists have not made up their minds just what it means. Then there is the matter of the little seals, made of baked clay. They were incised with patterns as if they had been made to stamp designs on something. There are whorls reminiscent of the whorls in a human fingerprint; there are patterns of human hands, and of rosettes, and of geometric designs. The little clay seals bear no trace of dye as they are found today, but probably organic vegetable dyes, the only ones available to those long-ago ancestors, would have left no trace anyway. Archaeologists don't know whether the people of Çatal Hüyük used them to dye cloth, or perhaps to dye the human body for certain unknown ceremonial occasions. No samples of dyed cloth have been found in the ruins, but some of the wall paintings repeat the patterns of the seals. Did the people at one time dye cloth to cover the walls, and did cloth take the place of wall painting itself at a later era? The answer hasn't yet come from the remains of the old city. Diggers did find a painted figure of a goddess whose body was covered with the same patterns as the seals. This rather implies that perhaps the people painted their own bodies, as certain African tribes and the American Indians and maybe even those Druids in England used to paint themselves.

Much clearer is the kind of thing the people of Çatal Hüyük regarded as treasure. For they, like many people who followed them, put important objects into the tomb with the dead so that they would have them handy in the next world. Weapons were almost always included in graves of men—polished maceheads of white marble, obsidian daggers, javelin heads. Some daggers are exquisitely worked, with handles of carved bone. Men wore "hook-and-eye" clothing fasteners of carved bone or of bits of antler, and these were often buried with them and found near the waist of the skeleton. Men also wore decorative necklaces of the teeth of wild animals, and wrist guards of bone. It was too early for armor, but they had learned to wear protective clothing of heavy woven cloth and leather.

Babies were buried with the little spoons their mothers had used to feed them, spoons often made from the ribs of wild cattle. Near the shoulders of the women, archaeologists found little bone pins which must have served to anchor their garments.

There were also bright obsidian mirrors and necklaces, and little packets of rouge still fully prepared for use after eight thousand years. The rouge was a vegetable dye mixed with fat, and it was kept in a small round basket. Beside it, in many graves, was another, slightly larger basket containing the mirror the lady no doubt used to study the effect.

Necklaces came in all sizes and shapes, and in all materials—copper, lead, mica, animal teeth, alabaster, white limestone. In a long report in *Anatolian Studies*, the Journal of the British Institute of Archaeology at Ankara, for 1964, James Mellaart points out that "Dentalium shell from the Mediterranean was cut into tubes or small slices, and cockle, whelk and freshwater shells were sliced and strung. Cowries [small sea shells with a high gloss, used as money by some peoples of Asia and Africa] were rare, but mother-of-pearl was frequent." The implication is clear: Çatal Hüyük lies more than 100 miles from the nearest sea, over mountains and rugged terrain. In 6500 B.C. it would have been a perilous trip of weeks or months to get to the sea and back. Yet the shells were made into jewelry in the town. Its people must, before the dawn of recorded history, have had a vigorous trade with seafaring people, or it must have sent its own young stalwarts down to the sea to trade the precious obsidian from their magic mountain for the precious goods of other people.

Most remarkable of all the finds of Çatal Hüyük, are the figurines and the wall paintings of the shrines. The figurines began, in the lowest and most primitive levels of the city, with bits of native rock that already were reminiscent of a human or animal figure. The early sculptor must have picked up such stones, stared at them, got an idea, and added eyes and mouth, or nose and eyes. Some are as powerful as the earth itself, blunt, enigmatic, very impressive. The earliest of all represent the Great Mother, a female figure often with enormous breasts and stomach. Her son is often shown as an animal. Nine thousand, eight thousand years ago, the overriding preoccupation of man was simple survival—finding a food supply and then sustaining and increasing it. The greatest divinity of his pantheon thus had to be the female figure, the Great Mother, source of all life. The little lumps of stone that emerge from Çatal Hüyük hold in them one of the first glim-

Hundreds of little clay mother-goddess figures with pendulous breasts and bulging stomachs were found at Çatal Hüyük during its excavation.

One of the first real wall paintings ever made by man is the great bull mural from Çatal Hüyük. The bull is painted in red on a cream-colored background and is surrounded by little stick figures of men with hunting instruments, and smaller animals. The bull is 6 feet long, and because of his huge size relative to that of the men, archaeologists believe that the mural depicts a scene of ritual worship rather than hunting.

merings of religious thought, and the past must truly run from the Great Mother to the Virgin Mary.

In addition to the sculptures are the great wall paintings, now celebrated by scholars as "man's first murals." They were put on the walls with some kind of brush, in a freehand application of color against a previously prepared white or cream-colored plaster. The artists had an astonishing range of colors—red, pink, black, buff, white, even mauve. They portrayed themselves and their fellow men, and they painted people a reddish color, as indeed they must have been, under that fierce sun. Most of the men seem to be dressed in a sort of stylized leopard-skin girdle with the spots of the leopard carefully painted. They are small figures in most energetic action: hunting, dancing, doing acrobatics, beating drums. Hunting scenes are spectacular, as men with bows and arrows, javelins, and knives swarm around beautifully executed stags with spreading antlers. Then there are the bulls: magnificent paintings often more than 6 feet long, with tiny stick-figures of men surrounding them. These scenes, and the hunting scenes, are reminiscent of cave paintings found at Lascaux, in southern France—paintings now dated to 20,000 B.C. Similar ones have turned up in the Sahara, dating from about 8000 to 3000 B.C., and the world still does not know what, if any, connection there is among the examples of this prehistoric art. It seems more likely that the urge to draw strikes all peoples, and the most natural thing to draw is the ordinary life of the day.

Some Çatal Hüyük shrines had paintings of leopards standing head to head and covered with decorative rosettes instead of their more naturalistic spots. Some had geometric designs repeated over and over, and some had what appear to be stylized human figures, seated, with both arms and legs raised at the sides in a position that is highly decorative but would be physically impossible for a modern human being to achieve. Perhaps the figures are of gods and goddesses, instead of real people, and the posture is one only the gods can attain.

By far the most common, after the Mother Goddess, is the bull's head as religious ornament. The bull too belonged to the fertility cult, and real horns or clay replicas of horns decorated not only shrines but also houses. A fine example of a Çatal Hüyük house, now dramatically exhibited in the Archaeological Museum of Ankara, has four sets of bulls' horns set into a well below a rock-cut relief of one of those arms-and-legs-up god figures, and above them both a tiny niche open to the outside air. Along all the walls are simple geometric designs in red, white, and black.

What happened, then, to the people of Çatal Hüyük and to their city? It flourished for a thousand years, and then it died. At the very lowest levels of excavation, down where the mud huts were built in 6500 B.C. or earlier, there was no sign of violent

James Mellaart with a plaster reproduction of a strange symbol found frequently in Çatal Hüyük—a seated figure with its arms and legs in a strange upright position. This may be a goddess or a talisman to ward off evil and bring good luck.

destruction. Here apparently, early man lived as long as he could, in the midst of his own mess, and then he filled in the living space and built a clean new house on top of the old one. The town grew quite rapidly in this period, became first rich, then congested. At the end of Level VIa, about 5800 B.C., there was a violent, disastrous destruction of still unknown origin. Slowly the town grew up again, grew prosperous, and was destroyed repeatedly by fire. There is no evidence of sacking here, of invasion by another people. Somebody's hearth fire must have blazed out of control and set fire to the timbers that were set into the mud walls for support, and the whole closely knit town burned up. Near the very top of the mound, at about 5600 B.C., there are signs of a fire but also of a man-made disturbance: shrines knocked about, bones disturbed, pots upended. Who did that? Who was around in 5600 B.C. to upset Çatal Hüyük? Archaeologists have found evidence of Greek pits and trenches in the ruins, and there are scraps of Roman-era pottery around. Were the Greeks and Romans hunting for treasure? The answer is still locked in the many mysteries of the life and death of the town called Çatal Hüyük.

Even in the midst of mystery, however, those modern magicians, the archaeologists, are able to find intriguing hints of the past. The people of this city, for example, were skillful cattle raisers who managed to raise and keep herds. Furthermore, they kept these semidomesticated animals on the edge of their town, in special pens and buildings. There were no pigs in the parlor in Çatal Hüyük, or chickens under the bed, as there still are today in many more "modern" societies. The early domesticated animals of Çatal Hüyük were smaller in size than their wild ancestors, probably because man didn't know quite how to care for his tame animals and didn't give them as much food as they could have found for themselves if they had not been in captivity.

How do we know all this? Today's archaeologists would no more go out armed only with a shovel and a pottery chart than a pilot would venture forth with nothing but an altimeter and a road map. An archaeological expedition today carries with it, or invites as temporary guests, experts, men and women equipped to deal with all the elements of human life: geologists who can trace the physical history of the terrain in which the ancients lived; botanists who can analyze seeds and plants and the traces of root patterns in the ravaged soil; anthropologists who can read volumes from old bones. The post-mortem on the fascinating story of the past is now approached as a many-faceted science.

Some astonishing facts emerge. What, for example, was the first animal domesticated by man? "The dog," most people would reply quickly, although a minority holds out for the horse. Both theories now appear to be wrong. From studies of animal bones at ancient city sites, it seems that sheep came first under the influence of man. A pair of Columbia University archaeologists named Ralph and Rose Solecki found sheep bones in carbon at a site in Iraq and managed to date them to about 9000 B.C. This makes the sheep the earliest known domesticated animal. The dog, though ousted from first place, still seems to have been the second pet of the human family; then the goat, then the pig, and somewhere between 5000 and 4000 B.C. the cow and the bull. The horse is still waiting in line.

Each dig, each cautious, probing theory raises a new batch of questions. In the justly famous recent ruins of Pompeii, in Italy (A.D. 79), archaeologists could determine what plants grew in gardens by pouring plaster of Paris down into the ancient root patterns and then analyzing the casts. At Çatal Hüyük this was impossible, and a botanical detective named Hans Helbaek, from Denmark, undertook a study of carbonized grain and seeds dug out of the ruins by Mellaart's crew. It was a job that would have staggered a lesser man, but Helbaek was beside himself with excitement because the blackened bits from the excavation were "the largest and best preserved finds of their kind ever recovered from so early periods in the Old World."

After months of work, Helbaek announced that the people of Çatal Hüyük had already domesticated some forms of wheat for bread, some barleys, some peas. They also gathered weeds because they had found the seeds useful in their diet. Man the roving hunter couldn't survive as man the city dweller and mural painter and occasional thinker until he could feed both himself and the animals he found useful, so the conscious cultivation of crops is an enormous step in the long, long journey. Helbaek found grains of two types of oily weed seeds in the remains of the town, and he concludes that the residents had learned to gather them as sources of fat and oil, like linseed oil or sesame, cottonseed, and the like. They had acorns, and they had almonds, both highly edible, and they ate pistachio nuts without paying the extravagant prices this delectable delicacy commands today in exotic-food stores.

They also picked some weeds apparently just for fun. Helbaek found seeds of two spiky grasses which were completely inedible but which must have made fine decorations for the inside of the houses. So the next question comes: who had time to pick things for mere decoration, the servants or the ladies of these old mud houses?

For decades, experts have known that a primitive form of barley, called einkorn, was present in prehistoric Europe as a basic human food source. But they never knew how it got to Europe. Among the seeds and grains Helbaek studied in Çatal Hüyük were unmistakable traces of this breed. It was a primitive form of the grain, but it was a cultivated form. Einkorn was raised deliberately, carefully in this place eight thousand years ago. Obviously, then, prehistoric Europe got it from Turkey. But where did Çatal Hüyük get it? The plant that is the ancestor of einkorn does not exist on the Anatolian plain and does not turn up as a weed in any of the carbonized remnants in the old city. The patient Hans Helbaek has answered one question only to be confronted by another one.

Perhaps even that answer is there, on the dusty hillside with the lone guard and his rifle. It may not be found for years. In 1965, excavator Mellaart started a trench below the lowest level of the old city and had to abandon it because water from the nearby irrigation ditches was seeping in. He still had not reached virgin soil—that is, soil untouched by human construction and habitation. How much farther down are the traces of man? Excavation at Çatal Hüyük stopped in 1965 and has never been resumed. All because, say the Turks, of "that Dorak business."

10

THAT DORAK BUSINESS

It began like a spy thriller, on a train going from Istanbul to
Izmir. Turkish trains, like most European trains, are equipped
with separate compartments instead of long open coaches in the
American style. In one compartment sat the young, bespectacled,
slightly plump archaeologist James Mellaart. He was reading, as
he always did on journeys. When the door to his compartment
opened, he hardly looked up. A young woman came in, closed
the door, and sat down opposite him. It was her bracelet, not her
face, that caught his eye. The bracelet was solid gold, and it was
made in a style Mellaart recognized as similar to the bracelets of
Troy.

Abruptly he closed his book, smiled politely into the young
lady's eyes, and began a tentative conversation. He had to know
where that bracelet came from. After a suitable interval of aim-
less talk, he asked her.

It came from home, she said diffidently. It was part of a collection of antiquities that she and her family owned. It was not
uncommon in Turkey for families to buy and collect ancient
objects. By now Mellaart's archaeological instincts were all
aquiver. Could he, he asked, possibly see the rest of the collection?

The girl, who called herself Anna, seems to have agreed quite amiably, although Mellaart was a stranger to her and it was already dark when the train reached Izmir. From the railroad station the two took a taxi to a pier, rode a ferryboat across the Izmir harbor, then took another taxi to Anna's house in a narrow street. Either because it was dark or because he was too excited over the treasure hoard to think of anything else, Mellaart did not notice either the name of the street or the route they took to arrive there.

By his own account, he spent the entire evening there talking, talking, talking to Anna as she opened a chest of drawers and brought out her treasures one by one. They were dusty, Mellaart recalls, as if seldom brought into the air, and each rested on its own bed of cotton. There were gold and silver figurines, a dagger almost a foot long made of silver covered with embossed gold, two black obsidian beakers, drinking cups of pure gold, some fragments of ancient textile.

Mellaart was stunned by the size and value of the collection. Cautiously, as if afraid that one false question would make both gold and girl vanish with a magician's *poof*, he asked what she knew about the origin of the items. At this, Anna produced two faded photographs of skeletons in shallow tombs, and a heap of closely written notes written in modern Greek. Anna translated the notes. The treasure had been found, she said, in some royal tombs of the ancient and mysterious Yortan culture in northwestern Turkey just south of the Sea of Marmara, near a town called Dorak. It had been dug up just after World War I when the Greeks and Turks were fighting their own extension of that conflict in Aegean Turkey.

The Yortan civilization was familiar to Mellaart. It had been a neighbor of Troy, and various objects had appeared on the international market from its tombs. Most had been relatively simple, however; no royal tomb had ever been found.

It was almost dawn on that summer night in 1958 before Mellaart could bear to take his eyes off the treasure, and Anna quite sensibly suggested that he stay there instead of trying to find a taxi and a hotel at that hour. Mellaart stayed for several days, sleeping, as he recalls, "in a first floor room at the back, overlooking a garden." He never left the house and he never saw anyone else, though he later said that he was sure there had been an older man somewhere in the house, probably Anna's father.

Repeatedly he asked if he could photograph the treasure, and Anna always refused. She did agree to let Mellaart make meticulous sketches and notes, however, and she promised that she would give him permission to publish an article about the wonderful find. If she could find a way to have photographs made without attracting too much attention, she would do so. Thus, one early morning Mellaart packed up his notes and his sketches, and before dawn slipped out of the house and back to the railroad station to return to his home in Istanbul. He scribbled down the name and address Anna gave him: Anna Papastrati, 217 Kazim Direk Street, Izmir.

From Istanbul, Mellaart went to Ankara to his job as assistant director of the British Institute of Archaeology. For weeks he told no one of his find. Later he explained that he was waiting for the photographs from Anna, to prove to his associates that he really had seen a fantastic and previously unknown Yortan hoard. When the pictures didn't come, he went to the British Institute's director, Seton Lloyd, and told him the whole story—with one notable deception thrown in almost gratuitously: he told Lloyd that he had run across the collection six years earlier, in 1952, but that he had been asked to keep quiet about it. Just why he invented this tale is not clear, although the most obvious reason would seem to be that he had been married for four years to a Turkish woman named Arlette Cenani, and perhaps he didn't want to try to explain to her what he had been doing all those days in Anna's house in Izmir. If the whole episode had happened in 1952, it would have been well before his marriage.

Whatever the reason, that was the first story Mellaart told. Twice during the summer of 1958 he wrote to Izmir asking about the promised photographs. There was no reply.

Then in mid-October a single sheet of ordinary note paper arrived in Ankara addressed to James Mellaart, Ingiliz Arkeoloji Enstitusu. The entire document read as follows:

> Miss Anna Papastrati
> Kazim Direk Caddesi, no. 217
> Karsyaka—Izmir
> 16/10/1958

Dear James,

Here is the letter you want so much. As the owner, I authorize you to publish your drawings of the Dorak objects, which you drew in our house. You always were more interested in these old things than in me.

Well, there it is. Good luck and goodbye.

> Love
> Anna Papastrati (signature)

The tone of the letter was very odd. Anna seemed to be deliberately hinting that there had been more to their relationship than the study of a treasure in antiquities. And she seemed at great pains to provide a document giving her name and address, something Mellaart could show if anyone questioned him. Yet she sent no photographs; indeed, she didn't even mention them.

At this point Seton Lloyd was in London, and he had shown Mellaart's sketches to archaeological colleagues and art historians, all of whom agreed that the material looked authentic and should be published. Anna's letter seemed to remove the last obstacle to publication, so the material, with an article by James Mellaart, went to the *Illustrated London News*, a magazine of high repute and one that regularly publishes long articles of archaeological interest. The article appeared on November 28, 1959, with several pages of Mellaart's meticulous drawings and a headline that was downright breathless for the sober *Illustrated London News*: THE ROYAL TREASURE OF DORAK—FIRST AND EXCLUSIVE REPORT OF A CLANDESTINE EXCAVATION WHICH LED TO THE MOST IMPORTANT DISCOVERY SINCE THE ROYAL TOMBS OF UR.

One of the most exciting items found in the royal tombs, Mellaart explained in his article, was a wooden chair or throne which was plated with thick sheets of gold on which had been embossed Egyptian hieroglyphs. The hieroglyphs were readable and bore the name and titles of the second king of the Fifth Egyptian Dynasty, Sahure, 2478–2473 B.C. Mellaart offered the opinion that the throne had been a royal gift from the Egyptian king to the Yortan king, and he wrote excitedly that "This . . . is the first piece of evidence of contact between the seafaring population of North-West Anatolia and Egypt in the third millennium B.C."

Although Mellaart had scrupulously informed the Turkish Department of Antiquities that he had come across a rich collection of the Yortan culture, and that he intended to publish an article on it shortly, the actual publication put the Turkish officials into an uproar never matched again until 1970's "Boston Museum hoard." There were immediate charges that Mellaart had smuggled the treasure out of Turkey; there were hints that he had actually dug it up himself, in secret at night.

Mellaart then told the Turks the whole story, and instantly a search began for the mysterious Anna Papastrati. She could not be found. The address she had given Mellaart, said the Turkish police, was in the commercial part of Izmir and there were no private homes there. Later it turned out that there are at least two Kazim Direk streets in the city, and street names are changed so often that it could have been almost anywhere. Mellaart's Turkish father-in-law, Kadri Cenani, sent a blank sheet of paper in a registered letter to "Anna Papastrati, Kazim Direk Caddesi 217," and got it back marked "The addressee was asked for at 217 Kazim Direk Street but the above-named was unknown there." This effort to help Mellaart did not produce the girl, but it certainly proved that the address existed, somewhere in Izmir, and was known to the mailman if not to the police.

Not only had Anna vanished; the hoard had vanished with her. Turkish authorities kept a sharp eye on Swiss antiquities dealers and on parcels going over their borders. Museums and archaeologists were alerted all over the world to watch out for the Dorak treasure. Mellaart told, over and over again, that he knew nothing about Anna except her address. She had spoken good English, he said, with an American accent, so he surmised that perhaps she worked for the United States Information Service in Izmir or for the NATO base with its hundreds of Americans. This was in a way an ominous sign, since everyone knew that the Army Post Office and a nearby military airfield were suspect as outlets for illegal export of antiquities.

By 1961 Mellaart was hard at work excavating his new site at Çatal Hüyük, and he clearly hoped that the whole affair would blow over and be forgotten. It was not to be. In late May, 1962, almost four years after Mellaart had seen the Dorak treasure and two and a half years after his article on it had appeared in London, one of Turkey's leading newspapers launched a sort of Holy Crusade against him. In the summer of 1971 a Turkish friend of mine pulled out yellowed copies of those old papers and read me the startling headlines: "An historic royal treasure worth a milliard lire smuggled out." A milliard lire is at today's rate of exchange worth more than $66 million. In 1962 it was worth about $100 million. Later issues of the same newspaper told of a Dorak villager who had seen a "fair-haired, fat foreigner" with a woman in the vicinity of the Dorak tombs in 1955 or 1956, and one account claimed that a village boy, shown a photograph of Mellaart, identified him unequivocally as the "fat foreigner."

In 1964 the uproar had become so fierce in Turkey that Mellaart was forbidden permission to dig at Çatal Hüyük, and in 1965 he was permitted to return only if some other British official was technically in charge of the dig and Mellaart acted as "assistant." The Turkish government increased the number of guards at the site, and Mellaart charged that they even had two special spies assigned to him, disguised as servants. Eventually the impatient archaeologist lost his temper completely, fought with his crew, and wrote a most indiscreet letter to one of the museums that helped finance his work. In it he complained bitterly about the Turks, compared one of the guards to the "Gestapo," and pointed out that it was extremely difficult to dig "in this cloak and dagger atmosphere."

That, apparently, was the last straw. From that moment until today, the name of James Mellaart has been invoked every time there is a new archaeological scandal or mystery in all of Turkey. In 1970 he was interviewed about "the Boston Museum hoard" and what he knew about it. He is constantly beset by the international press—any who can penetrate his security at his home in Istanbul, that is—each time a treasure either appears or disappears.

He has defenders, of course. The police chief of Izmir, who spent months looking for the mysterious Anna Papastrati, once declared that "In the absence of any proof, Mellaart must be considered innocent"—but that didn't help much. Two British journalists, Kenneth Pearson and Patricia Connor, spent months in Turkey trying to untangle the whole complicated story, and published an intriguing book in 1968 called *The Dorak Affair*. They too tried to find Anna and failed. They were offered priceless antiquities at virtually every site they visited, and they were alternately harassed and helped by the police. They trekked to the Dorak area and interviewed a man who said he had been quoted as having identified Mellaart as the mysterious stranger of 1955 or 1956. But, the man said, he had been misquoted by the Turkish newspaper. He had *not* made a positive identification because he was far from sure.

By 1964 it was perfectly clear that the Turkish police had given up trying to find anything positive with which to charge James Mellaart, and by 1965 the whole question was academic anyway because that year the Turkish Parliament passed an amnesty law that automatically dropped all court cases in the country dealing with foreigners.

Yet Mellaart, the man who once said, "I don't get on with people, but give me a site and just let me dig. That's all I ever need," has not been permitted to dig since 1965. In the summer of 1970 I asked a high Turkish government official when, if ever, the excavation at Çatal Hüyük would be recommenced. "I don't know," the man said moodily. "The best neolithic scholar in the world is James Mellaart, and he . . ." My official never finished the sentence. His voice drifted off, and then he said half under his breath, "It is a loss for Turkey."

What could be the answer to "that Dorak business"?

There are as many theories as there are archaeologists, though most of them seem to trust James Mellaart. Nobody but the wild-eyed Turkish press ever seemed to believe that Mellaart had found the treasure, dug it up himself, and then tried to invent the preposterous story of the girl on the train.

Was the whole thing, perhaps, a hoax? A man of Mellaart's knowledge and talent could have invented it all, including the girl. But why? In 1958 he was not the famous figure he became after the stunning digs at Hacilar and Çatal Hüyük; but he was highly respected by his peers, and he was on his way to the kind of achievement that is rare even in his exotic field. He didn't need a fake "find" to draw attention to himself.

There remains one more possibility: that the whole story was true as Mellaart told it, but that the girl Anna Papastrati was some kind of double agent in the whole tangled, murky network of the illegal traffic in antiquities. The police chief of Izmir once advanced this theory himself, saying it could have been no accident that she happened to run across the archaeologist on the train. It could, say many experts, have happened like this: Unscrupulous dealers got together a collection of valuable items from illegally excavated Yortan-culture tombs in or near Dorak. Having assembled their hoard, they realized that the items were rare enough to be considered fake unless they had some reputable expert vouch for them. But a reputable expert, if approached openly, might denounce them and ruin the sale. Mellaart was known as one of the leading authorities in the field, and he was further known to be a man with such a passion for antiquity that he would rush headlong to investigate any item that crossed his path. Colleagues describe him as "impetuous," "obsessed," "sometimes indiscreet." Just the man for the job. If one accepts this theory, it was easy enough for the dealers to find Anna, plant her on the train wearing a solid-gold bracelet, and wait for Mellaart to snap at the bait. Whether the ploy of her taking him "home" with her was an attempt to compromise him or not can never be known, but it hardly matters. Once Mellaart had seen the treasure, he would burn to report it to the world, and this he did. The "Dorak treasure" achieved instant fame through one publication in one magazine.

So far as it goes, this theory seems the most logical. But then what happened to the treasure so carefully, so skillfully, presented to the world of prospective buyers? How could it have vanished? One American archaeologist who has worked in Turkey ventured an explanation to me, but requested that his name not be used: he, like all the others, fears to speak about "that Dorak business" for fear of losing his own permission to work in Turkey.

"There are warped souls in the world who like to buy valuable collections and then hide them, to gloat in private like Silas Marner and his gold," the archaeologist said to me. "I do not believe Jimmy Mellaart is one of those, so I do not believe he has the treasure or that he even knows where it is. I do not believe it is in the hands of a museum, because it is too hot now for any museum to handle. If it ever existed, and I am tempted to believe that it did, I believe it was smuggled out, perhaps even before Jimmy published on it, and that after publication it was sold to a private collector. But I have no proof whatever."

His phrase "if it ever existed" hung in the air even after he had stopped speaking. I didn't think much about it at the time— but then came the late summer of 1971 and a whole new mystery which touched James Mellaart's work once again: the business of the "Hacilar forgeries."

11

THE HACILAR FORGERIES

Just before World War II—twenty years before the great early–Bronze Age site of Beycesultan had been excavated by Seton Lloyd and James Mellaart, and more than twenty years before Mellaart made his stunning neolithic discoveries at Hacilar and Çatal Hüyük—some oddly shaped but lovely little pots and figurines began to drift into the world's art and antiquities markets from an unknown site in Turkey. Eagle-eyed Swiss dealers snapped them up from sources in Istanbul, in Ankara, in Izmir, and Turkish dealers passed them along to favorite customers.

By the middle 1950s, knowledgeable dealers had located the source somewhere near the modern Turkish town of Burdur, in the southwestern part of the country. Then a peasant plowing in a field about 15 miles from Burdur turned up some pottery of the chalcolithic era (about 5000 to 3000 B.C.), a beige color with fine red painted designs. Instantly, illegal excavators hurried to the peasant's land and conducted their own clandestine operations, feeding the pots into an ever-growing world market. It was this illicit traffic which attracted Mellaart's attention to the site in the first place. He began excavating in 1957 on the site we now know as Hacilar, and under the chalcolithic level he found a neolithic town whose art and architecture foreshadowed the even more spectacular finds at Çatal Hüyük. Mellaart dug for four seasons, from 1957 through 1960, and turned his finds over to the Turkish government. Many of them are visible today in the Archaeological Museum at Ankara. But a great many more "Hacilar figurines" and "Hacilar vases" are scattered in museums from New York City to Paris to London and in dozens of private collections all over the world.

It is axiomatic in the archaeological world that once a legitimate excavation begins, the diggers get enormous amounts of unrequested and undesired help from the entire surrounding countryside. Most digs in Turkey are conducted for only a few months each year, and when the legal excavators leave, the robbers move in. It simply costs too much to guard the sites adequately, and in Turkey as in Italy, Greece, Guatemala, some guards are bribable and the local peasants are canny and patient.

After Mellaart and his crew removed everything they could and left the Hacilar site in 1960, there was so much clandestine activity that the Turkish authorities actually bulldozed the site to close excavation holes and discourage the sticky-fingered natives. Still, the flow of "Hacilar pottery" continued. In 1962 some pottery typical of the area turned up at the prestigious auction firm of Sotheby's in London. The Metropolitan Museum in New York bought a figurine in the early 1960s which it exhibited proudly in a 1966 Near Eastern art exhibition. Oxford University's Ashmolean Museum in England bought three bowls; the Louvre in Paris, a museum in Berlin, and another in Geneva acquired pieces of the precious art.

The British journalists Pearson and Connor, while in Turkey in their pursuit of the truth in "that Dorak business," were offered a "genuine Hacilar goddess" for a bargain price of $560. It would truly have been a bargain: single pieces from this site have brought literally thousands of dollars each.

"Hacilar pottery is very pretty stuff," said James Mellaart recently; "that's why everybody wants a bit of it."

It was his theory that the sudden flood of Hacilar figurines and bowls and pots on the market in the '60s came from the clandestine discovery of the cemetery of the old city.

This 7,000-year-old vase from Hacilar, with a reddish pattern painted on white-beige clay, is owned by the Ankara Archaeological Museum and is believed to be authentic. Many pieces like it, however, sold to other museums or to private collectors, are forgeries which were exposed in August, 1971, by a team of British investigators.

For all its similarities to Çatal Hüyük, Hacilar (7000 to 5000 B.C., roughly) did not reveal burials inside the homes, under the platforms. A few skeletons were found in houses, but nothing like the number found in Çatal Hüyük. From this, Mellaart had concluded that Hacilar had a cemetery somewhere outside its walls. He didn't find it in the excavation period 1957–60, and he did not go back to look again. It seemed logical to him, and to many other archaeologists and dealers and museum directors, that the new Hacilar material must be coming from this cemetery.

Then suddenly, in early August of 1971, British archaeological detectives hurled a bombshell into the international market. In an article in the scientific magazine *Archaeometry*, three distinguished scholars announced that they had tested 66 objects of "Hacilar" ware and found that 48 of them were fakes. Among them was a stunning double-headed "anthropomorphic" vase (the word means "having the attributes of human form"; in this case, the little vase was pointed at the bottom and swelled into an almost-human figure with two heads bearing human features), bought by the Ashmolean Museum in 1965, plus all three of the little bowls it had purchased earlier. Five "Hacilar" pieces from the British Museum were fakes, the report said, 12 from a collection in Switzerland, at least one from New York's Metropolitan Museum of Art, and several from private collections.

At first there was a stunned silence from the museums and the individuals. No one likes to be deceived, least of all scholarly institutions. In addition to this blow to their pride, most had paid high prices for art that was now virtually valueless. "I am sorry," said a spokesman for the British Museum, "that public money has been spent on these things."

The first suspicion about the fake Hacilar pieces apparently came to Dr. Peter Ucko of the University College of London. In 1962 he saw a Hacilar figurine at Sotheby's auction house, and something about the style of it disturbed him. The piece belonged to a New York agent who had bought it, along with about 25 other items, from a Swiss dealer. He was offering it for sale at Sotheby's. Dr. Ucko looked at it closely, doubted its authenticity, but had no way of testing it or proving anything. "Stylistic evidence alone was not at that point generally accepted," he said later.

About three years later another expert, Dr. Martin Aitken of the research laboratory for archaeology and the history of art at Oxford University, became suspicious of the Ashmolean Museum's double-headed vase and three bowls. Most museums and reputable dealers like to test bits of antiquity before they buy them, for both moral and financial reasons. Dr. Aitken tested the Ashmolean's new purchases and matched them against some sherds (fragments of pottery) which the Turkish government gave him from Mellaart's legal dig at Hacilar. He didn't like the results he got, but he explained late in 1971 that when he did the tests in 1965 he "felt unable, at the time, to condemn [the Ashmolean purchases] unequivocally."

One man who shared Dr. Aitken's slight discomfort about the vase and the bowls was Dr. Roger Moorey of the Ashmolean itself. Quietly, he and Aitken went about now testing with even newer methods. In the meantime, Dr. Ucko went on with his patient analysis of stylistic differences between the articles in museums and those confirmed as genuine on the site of the Hacilar dig and at the Ankara museum. The devastating report of August, 1971, was signed by all three men.

For years, archaeologists had to rely upon near-guesswork to determine the age of the artifacts they turned up from the earth. They made careful analyses of the style of vases, bowls, statues, and the degree of skill they exhibited in workmanship. They compared vases from one ancient site with those from another; they read ancient histories and translated inscriptions and painstakingly assigned and then reassigned dates to the objects they dug up.

Nowadays, however, all the tools of modern science help them out. Cameras originally created to fly in the U-2 spy planes have been adapted to look for lost and buried cities, using special film that detects, by the color of the vegetation, areas of buried brick and stone. Magnetometers designed for space research are used to locate ancient masonry. A complex potassium-argon dating system, sometimes called an "atomic clock," can establish the age of rocks billions of years old.

One of the most reliable, and best-known, of modern dating systems is the measurement of radiocarbon. The system is most commonly called Carbon-14 dating, and it is accurate, give or take a hundred years, back to about seventy thousand years ago. It is based upon the fact that all living things absorb tiny amounts of radioactive carbon, created by cosmic rays, from the atmosphere itself. When an organism dies, its stored-up Carbon-14 begins to disintegrate. The rate at which it disintegrates has been clearly established, so all the detective needs to do is measure the proportion that remains and he knows how long ago the organism died. Carbon-14 has been used on bones, plant seeds, any number of once-living organisms that are found in tombs and

ancient city sites, to establish the age of the archaeological artifacts beside or near them.

In exposing the Hacilar forgeries, however, the art detectives
used primarily another technique known as the thermolumines-
cence. This is a technique for measuring the amount of light that
has built up in the form of electrons trapped in the clay since the
moment it was fired. The measurement makes it perfectly clear
whether the pottery in question was fired long ago or only quite
recently. In the case of the Hacilar fakes, 48 of the 66 tested had
been fired "recently."

To be doubly and triply sure, however, the scientists also tested
the Hacilar pieces by a method of optical spectrography which
breaks down and analyzes the spectrum of colors and dyes used.
Then they threw in an examination of the mineral content just
for good measure.

The latter turned out to be fascinating. Virtually every one of
the pots and vases tested had some slight surface incrustation,
like the moss or lichen on an old tree. Some pots had a gray
incrustation; others showed rather white. Mineral analysis revealed that the gray crust was calcareous, or chalky, very like the
soil found around Hacilar. The white crust, however, was soft
and noncalcareous. It could not have been acquired naturally in
Hacilar, and thus must be some clue as to where and how the
forgeries were made.

British and American museums, and Turkish authorities themselves, cooperated eagerly in the long investigation that revealed
the fakes. The Turks, despite their general displeasure with the
international art market, were delighted to help expose the
scandal, and the Ankara Archaeological Museum sent along fragments of six figurines from its own collection for comparison with
the questioned pieces.

Interestingly, the nonscientific and purely stylistic judgments
that Dr. Ucko had made independently of the survey turned out
to be completely accurate. He did not miss on a single piece. On
the basis of this success, he now believes that some of the Hacilar-
style figurines in the Louvre in Paris, in private collections, and
even in the Ankara Museum itself must be fakes. In Ankara, a
government archaeologist waved his hand at a showcase with

about twenty Hacilar-style objects and said flatly, "All fakes. We knew they were. The items we display in the rest of the Museum we know are genuine, because I was there when Mellaart's team dug them up."

Still unsolved at this writing is the mystery of who could have done the forgeries, and when. It seems likely they were made in Turkey and near to the Hacilar site, where the proper clay is available. One Swiss collector who was the middleman for many of the artifacts, both genuine and false, says that he made all his purchases *inside* Turkey. Ironically enough, this dealer bought one double-headed anthropomorphic Hacilar vase for himself, and this one seems to be genuine. It is now the only one known to be genuine in all the world, and as such it is worth more than $35,000.

Suspicion of forgery has fallen upon three faceless men: "the schoolmaster," "the peasant," and "the chauffeur." The schoolmaster is a man the Turkish government announced, early in 1971, had been "transferred to another area of the country" because he had been making fake antiquities of such a high standard that they fooled museums. Neither the schoolmaster's name nor the part of the country from which he was transferred was identified in the announcement, however. The peasant is also anonymous. He was brought up by an Ankara official as soon as the scandal broke. He had worked at the Hacilar dig during Mellaart's excavations, the official said, and since then he had been known to sell fake pottery from the site. The chauffeur is an even more mysterious and ominous character. He worked part time around Hacilar as a chauffeur in the era in which illegal pots first began appearing on the market. He is known to have done some digging on his own—it was his finds that attracted Mellaart's attention in 1956. The "chauffeur" had vanished from the area by the mid-1960s when reporters Pearson and Connor arrived on the scene, but the moment they began making inquiries about him the police picked them up. In an article that appeared in the summer, 1967, issue of *Horizon*, Mr. Pearson and Miss Connor wrote that "The newest apartment block in the town of Burdur, fifteen miles away, was built on the proceeds of the sale of Hacilar objects. This was stated by the police who picked us up for questioning in Burdur as soon as it was known that we were asking for a one-time chauffeur. . . . The chauffeur, the police claimed, had become a millionaire on the illegal sale of Hacilar artifacts."

If museum directors have nightmares, they must be full of horrendous visions of fakes and forgeries. Hardly a single institution in the world has escaped the wiles of the clever fakers, and some deceits have become resoundingly famous. In 1961 the British Museum in London presented an entire special exhibit of fakery which it had bought, over the years, believing the items to be genuine. In that same year the Metropolitan Museum of Art in New York admitted that three of its most famous figures, the great "Etruscan" terra-cotta warriors, dated from the fifth century B.C., had actually been created in the twentieth century by an enterprising trio of Italian pot-menders north of Rome.*

Often, museums keep, and continue to display, their famous fakes, but they carefully label them as forgeries for the edification of students. One Italian archaeologist, the Rumanian-born Dinu Adamesteanu, customarily builds cases inside new museums for the display of such work because he believes that "Museums should be an education for people."

The fate of the Hacilar fakes is still in doubt. Officials of the Ashmolean Museum have indicated that they would like "further tests" before they relegate their precious pots to the status of forgeries. A spokesman for the British Museum announced that it would keep its own. "They will be put aside for the instruction of future staff," he said. "I think that fakes should be collected, within reason, because it takes them out of circulation and stops them causing any more mischief."

At Sotheby's auction house an official said, "We simply do not sell Hacilar material any more. Too much has been proved to be forged. If any new pieces came in we certainly would test them, but we would give the buyer no warranty of genuineness."

Ironically, the police in most archaeologically rich nations know fairly well where forgeries are made, and in some cases

---

* For a full discussion of this famous forgery, see the author's previous book *Pots and Robbers*, published in 1970.

even who makes them. Thus a *carabiniere* colonel in Italy could remark a few years ago that "The best Etruscan *bucchero* is done at the moment in Gubbio, Italy, but the best 'early bronzes' are made right here in Rome." In Turkey, both police and archaeologists assured me that the "best fakes" come from the Burdur area, where the Hacilar items undoubtedly were created, and from the province of Hatay, near the Syrian border. Without adequate staff to guard the genuine treasures of the past, the police hardly have time to chase worthless fakes. In the illegal-antiquities market, it is the buyer who must beware.

Thus, on the day after the Hacilar-forgeries story broke, a Turkish journalist interviewed several men and women who were quietly studying objects in the Ankara Archaeological Museum. What did they think, he asked, about the scandal of forged antiquities in all these foreign museums?

The replies he got were unanimous: "It serves them right."

12

A LOST WHITE MARBLE CITY

In the late summer of 1970, the then-premier of Turkey, Mr. Suleyman Demirel, announced a sweeping devaluation of Turkish currency to combat inflation. "Free enterprise," he told his people, "must not degenerate into profiteering."

Within a month after this announcement, some American archaeologists digging away in a poplar grove near a village called Geyre, in southwestern Turkey, came upon a heap of stone tablets inscribed in Latin. There were more than 140 fragments, of various sizes, and as they lifted them carefully from the earth the excavators could make out the sense of the message. Even scholars occasionally get the giggles, and the diggers at Geyre all but rolled on the ground laughing. They had found an Edict on Maximum Prices issued by the Roman Emperor Diocletian in A.D. 301. Denouncing the merchants of the era as "avaricious," Diocletian said sternly that he could not allow "the Roman Empire to be turned into those venal things the merchants wish it to be." Thus in his capacity as "caretaker of all civilized and uncivilized peoples," he proceeded to establish rigid price controls on everything from linen and wool to cereal, ink, and egret feathers.

As they carefully pieced together the fragments, and counted their devalued Turkish lire, the archaeologists could only use a phrase Diocletian himself might have pronounced: *"Nihil novi sub sole"*—"There is nothing new under the sun."

When Diocletian's decree came, 1,700 years ago, to this poplar grove, the town was called not Geyre but Aphrodisias. It was 1,000 miles from Rome but still well within the empire's boundaries, and it was a big city. It stood in a beautiful wide valley near the slopes of Baba Dagh—"father mountain"—and though it was 100 miles from the Aegean sea, it was cool and well watered. Springs gushed from rocks and were channeled in stone-lined gutters to serve homes and public buildings. Almond trees, pomegranates, and poplars waved in the breeze. And Aphrodisias was a gleaming, glittering city of white marble set against the green. It had a stadium that could seat thirty thousand spectators; a theater; an enormous Temple of Aphrodite, the Greek goddess for whom the city was named. There had been people in Aphrodisias for three thousand years. The first were an indigenous Carian people, who probably called the place Ninoe. Then in the third century B.C., Alexander the Great swept through this part of Turkey, and waves of Greeks followed him. They named the city for their goddess, and by the first century of our era the Roman dictator Sulla considered the Carian Aphrodite so powerful that he sent her a golden crown and a double ax, hoping thus to enlist her aid in his affairs.

It was under later Roman rule, however, that Aphrodisias became famous throughout the empire. The mountains that sheltered the site are thick with deposits of magnificent marble—one variety an almost milky white, and other bluish with white veins through it. Rapidly, the young men of the city began to learn to shape the marble, and as years passed a school of sculpture grew. By the second and third centuries of the Christian Era the Aphrodisian sculptors were reputed to be the best in the world, and Roman emperors sent all the way to Aphrodisias to commission busts and statues, reliefs and friezes for the homes and public buildings of mighty Rome. Sometimes the sculptors themselves were summoned to the capital to work there; two of the dark gray marble centaurs still visible in the Capitoline Museum in

Rome are by Aphrodisian sculptors. In that age few artists signed their work, but the proud sculptors of Aphrodisias almost always did. More than thirty sculptors' names have been specifically identified.

Grand and handsome as were the pieces shipped abroad, the Aphrodisian artists saved their best work for their own city, and the legend of the beautiful white marble city was told in all the civilized world. Though it was severely damaged several times by earthquakes, and besieged by primitive tribes, Aphrodisias survived until the twelfth century, when it fell to invading Seljuk Turks. Then it vanished from history. Yet the memory of it lingered. During the Renaissance, the romantics dreamed of it, lost out there somewhere in mysterious Turkey, and some scholars believe that it was actually Aphrodisias which inspired the imaginary city of Calindra that Leonardo da Vinci wrote about in his account of a voyage to the Taurus Mountains. In the Elizabethan era, far-ranging sailors who bought statues in all the islands and seaports of the eastern Mediterranean talked about "lost Aphrodisias," but there is no record that they ever visited or found it. One intrepid traveler, the Englishman Richard Pococke, visited it about 1740 and wrote about its ruins. Then nothing. A French expedition reached it in 1904 and 1905, and the excavators loaded up some Aphrodisian marbles and carried them back to France to decorate their villas. An Italian expedition worked briefly at the site in 1937, but World War II halted its efforts.

By the 20th century, most of the city walls had fallen down, the theater was so full of rubble that it appeared to be an innocuous hillside, and only a few thin marble columns glittered among the poplars, looking, from a distance, like slightly thicker trees in the graceful grove. A raggle-taggle Turkish village named Geyre existed beside and on top of the ruins. Though it is only 100 miles from the bustling modern port city of Izmir (ancient Smyrna), Geyre is off the main road, and until the last decade virtually nobody went there. In 1956 another earthquake rattled the ruins and knocked down half the flimsy dwellings of Geyre, and the Turkish government in a relief program ordered everybody out and built a new village of Geyre two kilometers away. One day when the move had just begun, the villagers began digging a channel down the slopes of "father mountain" to bring water for their gardens, and on the edge of ancient Aphrodisias their picks and shovels rang against stone. They had come upon exquisitely cut marble blocks and sculptured friezes. Turkish archaeologists rushed to the site and persuaded the farmers to dig their ditches somewhere else. They gathered up the marble bits that had been exposed and locked them inside a ramshackle shed which must have been constructed to store surplus apples or garden goods.

Two years later, a peripatetic Turkish photographer named Ara Güler, from Istanbul, was in the nearest neighboring city of Aydin on business. Güler finds the villages more amusing than the small cities, so he went off aimlessly looking for a village in which to spend the night. "Chance took me to Geyre," he recalls. "I had never heard of it. And I couldn't believe my eyes. There were these magnificent columns, just standing there. I was astounded by the fragments of statues. There were columns lying around on the ground, and some of them had been propped up to support the sagging walls of the tumble-down village. There was a beautiful Greek-style carved sarcophagus being used as the central fountain of the village, and some of the farmers were playing cards on top of another one. I had never seen such a beautiful site. I rushed to get my cameras, and I took a lot of pictures and sent them to my agent in Paris. The agent showed them to the people from the American magazine *Horizon,* and they asked if I had taken any color pictures. I hadn't, but I assured them that I had, and then I drove all night to get back to Geyre and take color pictures. When the layout was made they asked me about a writer, so I went to the director of the Istanbul Archaeological Museum and I asked him who could write about Aphrodisias. He said he couldn't, but that he had a cousin or something in the United States who was an archaeologist and a teacher. His name was Kenan Erim. . . ."

Kenan T. Erim, Ph.D., a Turkish-born American citizen, teaches at New York University. He has beautiful dark Turkish eyes and a slightly bald head and enormous Dickensian sideburns, and he is a romantic. He had never seen Aphrodisias until 1959, but unlike photographer Güler, he knew all about it. "I

Two peasants from the hamlet of Geyre thresh grain by beating it with wooden mallets on top of a carved Greek marble sarcophagus.

*A marble column base holds up a sagging porch that is a favorite
lounging place for the villagers.*

had dreamed of Aphrodisias ever since my days at Princeton, where I was studying classical art and archaeology," he recalls. "I had a book written by an Italian scholar, Maria Floriani Squarciapino, who identifies Aphrodisias as the home of a very significant school of sculpture in the first centuries of the Christian Era. I couldn't wait to see it, and I had a dream that one day it would be mine."

In 1961 Professor Erim was there, with the financial support of the National Geographic Society, and he has worked there every summer since. He is now aided also by the Andrew W. Mellon Foundation, the Vincent Astor Foundation, and the Ford Foundation. No current "dig" in all of Turkey has been so rich in classical treasure as Aphrodisias, and the astounded Professor Erim can hardly believe his own good fortune. "Imagine a site where heads literally tumble out of walls into your hands!" he says.

It began the first day he was on the site. It was a hot day in 1961, and he had gone out, with the Turkish watchman, to have a look at that irrigation trench the villagers had started five years before. By this time it had filled with weeds, and Erim first squatted on a protruding marble block, then crawled down into the trench. As he raised his head, he stared almost straight into the face of a marble head. "I shouted to the photographer, and to the watchman, and then we all shouted at one another, 'Look, there's a marble head!' Latif the watchman actually lifted it out and handed it to me. It was beautiful, a woman's head with waved hair drawn to the nape of her neck. Her nose was broken, but otherwise she was intact, and she wore a curious headdress like a tiara but with sculptured shapes of towers and walls crowning it. This could mean only one thing: she was the personification of the city itself. All three of us walked over to the storeroom where the Turkish authorities had been putting things accidentally turned up at the site. I had this sort of nagging memory of a headless statue in there. It was a statue of a woman with flowing, wind-blown drapery, and it had no head. I walked straight to it, carrying my lady in my arms, and I lifted up the head and put it on top of the neck. It fitted. The breaks joined perfectly. It was as if she had come back to life. As beautiful as she was 1,700 years ago or more.

"But there was another little miracle that day. Latif was scrambling around in some of the boxes of fragments in the back of the room, and pretty soon he came out of the shadows carrying a piece of marble inscribed with traces of Greek letters. He lifted this fragment up and fitted it precisely into the side of the statue. The inscription on it said *Polis*—'the city.' It was a sign. Aphrodisias was ours."

Perhaps because he is so fond of talismans, Erim keeps finding them. On the last day of the 1970 dig, just before he and his crew packed up for the year, they were excavating in the ancient theater. This building, unlike the stadium, had been turned into a fortress in Byzantine times and then had totally collapsed. Erim and his fellow scholars had a hunch, however, that the theater had been destroyed by an earthquake even before its fortress days and that, therefore, there might be almost intact statues way down in the bottom layer of the ruin where they had fallen during the earthquake. Several seasons of patient earth-moving proved this theory correct. Day after day the reclaimed treasure piled up, but then on the last day out came a big, beautiful, idealized head which represented the people of the city of Aphrodisias.

"On my first day I found the city, and now on the last day of the last season, we found the people," says Erim. "It *must* be symbolic."

The site of Aphrodisias today is dreamlike. From Izmir the road is good, the only peril the *kamikaze* tactics of the truck drivers. Then one turns off at the provincial capital of Karacasu and it becomes a nightmare. Karacasu is paved with the most eccentrically set giant cobblestones ever to challenge an automobile's suspension system. If car, teeth, and nerves survive this jolting passage, the cobblestones yield to a twisting red-dirt road, redder even than the blood-colored hills of Spain, and then suddenly—there, off to the right—an almost hallucinating flash of white. Could they be columns? They are columns. This was the Greek agora, the market place. To the right the fourteen columns of the Temple of Aphrodite, which pious later Romans turned into a Christian church. There are the stadium, and the acropolis that was the heart of the city, and the gaping excavation of the

197

Aphrodisias as it looks today: in the background, the columns of the Temple of Aphrodite gleam in the sun.

theater. There is the enchanting little white marble *odeon* with its intimate tiers of seats and a deep pool in which perhaps there were once aquatic entertainments. There are the enormous baths of the Emperor Hadrian built for the Romans—who loved public bathing and, to judge by the number of huge baths they left behind, must have spent half their days lolling around in hot water. This building had central heating almost two thousand years ago, the heat from roaring wood fires circulating under a floor sup-

ported by terra-cotta pillars at the center. They could choose the room for bathing by the water temperature they preferred, and could finish off with a bracing dive into a cold pool. Entrance porticoes were decorated with heads 3 feet high—some bulls' heads, minotaurs, all the mythical monsters of the Roman world.

But most impressive of all is that ramshackle warehouse, surely the world's strangest museum. Stacked against the wall are the gleaming marble figures, some with heads, some in fragments. There are heads neatly arranged on the pounded-earth floor, and magnificent marble friezes leaning against the walls. There are boxes, cartons, shelves, loaded with fragments. And outside, too big to go into the overflowing warehouse, there are slender marble columns and ranks of sarcophagi. There is enough to fill two museums, and it stands oddly like the storeroom of a dusty film studio, or a properties shed for some great classical opera.

No one is allowed inside without an attendant, as the sight of such riches stirs larceny in the soul of even the scrupulous, and as yet Erim and the Turkish government have not been able to raise enough money to build a proper museum. Yet the place is haunting, unbelievable . . . all those people standing there, Artemis and Aphrodite, Apollo, Roman legionaires in their helmets, magistrates looking magisterial, philosophers, poets, boxers. There are wonderful boxers with broken noses and cauliflower ears, and a hilarious Hercules which must have been done as a spoof two thousand years ago. The famous muscle-man is shown all but tied in knots from the strain of performing one of his feats of strength, and his eyes are bugged out and almost crossed with the effort of it all.

As the earnest archaeologists go about their work, villagers from Geyre ride by on tiny donkeys, bundled to the eyes against the midday heat. They till the fields nearby, and their children peer solemnly at the foreigners hacking so carefully to clear the debris of centuries. The old houses of Geyre still stand in and near the excavation area, tilting more crazily with each passing year, and on still autumn afternoons one can stand in the Temple of Aphrodite and clearly hear the Moslem call to prayer from the thin minaret in the new village two kilometers away. The sarcophagus fountain still works in the old town, and bits of column still shore up the sagging porches. Erim intends not to move them so long as there is no proper museum to put them in, and until the villagers of Geyre decide not to keep coming back, nostalgically, to their pre-1956 houses.

The sarcophagi have a wonderful story all their own. Apparently with all that marble around, and with the Greek and Roman passion for handsomely carved burial coffins, the sculptors of Aphrodisias set up what was in effect a mail-order business. Rapidly they constructed and shaped the marble boxes, drilled holes to outline handsome reliefs on sides and top, and blocked out areas for heads to be added later. Then traveling salesmen roamed around the Roman world offering them for sale. Once the

A peasant and his laden donkey stride past ancient columns.

basic design and pattern had been indicated, local and presumably less-talented sculptors in other cities could finish the design and sculpt the customers' portraits into the blocked-out head areas. It was a brisk business.

One of the most popular sarcophagus designs featured clusters of grapes and the love god Eros frolicking among them. To the Turkish peasants the sarcophagi have always served as very handy wine presses, and for centuries they have happily plunked their grapes into the marble boxes, then climbed in after them to stamp out the juice.

"Even though I am of Turkish origin, and I can speak to them, I cannot convince them that these troughs are coffins, not wine presses," says Erim. "They listen to me politely, and then they laugh and shake their heads and point to the design of grapes carved into the marble. Obviously, they say, I am wrong. These were made for wine presses."

Perhaps because of the sheer beauty of the site, perhaps because of the personality of Kenan Erim, Aphrodisias each year is a singularly gratifying expedition. There are always university students there, learning archaeology by doing it. Ten in 1970 were on Ford Foundation grants; others either paid their own way and dug for bed and board or had other financial aid. The excavation is a fairly straightforward exploration of the now-familiar classical world, and Erim is a teacher as well as an archaeologist, so he likes to use the summer as a training course for his own students and others.

The expedition house is one of the sturdier of the peasant houses of old Geyre, and it has been made more livable by miles of mosquito netting and a garden. The National Geographic flag flaps gaily from a balcony, and a whimsical "No Peddlers" sign warns visitors to mind their manners. Erim conducts an informal seminar each night after work, and when that is finished the group often troops off to the exquisite little marble *odeon* for an informal concert of classical music on Erim's tape recorder.

"We always have flowers on the dining table at night, and when we have a glorious new head or a good find we put it in the middle of the table as a centerpiece, for a kind of celebration,"

Part of the beautiful little marble odeon *where archaeologist Kenan Erim and his students occasionally go at night for tape-recorded concerts on the little theater's marble seats.*

he says. "It's more civilized that way. Humanity should not get lost in a mass of charts and data and high scholarship. This was a city, with people in it, a city with style and beauty. Even the sunsets in Aphrodisias are more beautiful than elsewhere."

At the end of the last season, the expedition literally lived and ate with one of those citizens of old Aphrodisias. She is a colossal statue of a woman, almost 10 feet high, headless but with a handsomely carved garment which seems almost to be armor. "She was actually quite hard to handle," Erim recalls. "We tried to hoist her up with our tripod, but she broke the chain, so finally we just hauled her in and put her on her back in the expedition house. We've grown quite fond of having her there."

Outside, in the garden, there are statues everywhere wrapped in protective plastic and burlap. There are roses growing around the figures, and sarcophagi filled with flowers. "One day," says Erim dreamily, "we might even have grapes. . . . Aphrodisias lives again, in all her beauty."

13

EXCAVATIONS AT SEA

One of the delightful aspects of archaeology is the total unexpectedness of it all. Diggers find incredibly ancient frescoes in the mud ruins of a Çatal Hüyük, while the palaces of the far more "recent" Lydians have vanished. Simple terra-cotta jugs last centuries longer than the proud ships that carried them. Only traces remain of the Sardis refineries which helped produce the first real coinage of the world, and yet less than 100 miles south of Sardis one can still see strange bronze ingots, shaped like the skins of animals, which four thousand years ago became among the first known means of exchange other than barter in trade and commerce.

The ingots are exhibited in a unique Museum of Underwater Archaeology in the Turkish town of Bodrum. Bodrum was the ancient Halicarnassus, capital city of the country of King Mausolus, whose tomb was one of the Seven Wonders of the World. Mausolus has been gone for 2,300 years and his mausoleum for almost that long, though many of its stones and carvings are incorporated into a grand, turreted, romantic Crusader castle which dominates Bodrum and the deep blue of the Aegean Sea today. Inside the castle, in the museum, stand the ingots. They

A section of the Museum of Underwater Archaeology in Bodrum displays ancient amphorae of various kinds, taken from shipwrecks in the area.

The Crusader castle at Bodrum, now a museum, was built mainly with stones from the tomb of King Mausolus—the "mausoleum."

are so old that even Mausolus himself probably never saw one; certainly the Crusaders never even heard of them. Nor, I must confess, had I. They are lined up on supporting racks beside the beautiful Greek bronze heads fished from under the sea, near the shell-encrusted amphorae (clay jars) rescued from long-lost ships. Each ingot was 3 or 4 feet high and 2 or 3 inches thick, and each was shaped vaguely like an oxhide or a deerskin, with four strange iron "legs" attached. I puzzled over them for minutes, wondering if they could have been some kind of primitive armor plating for warships, until a friendly tourist lent me a dog-eared guidebook to the museum. The strange ingots, which had been known before only in Egyptian tomb paintings of the second mil-

In a courtyard of the castle, an anchor encrusted with marine deposits and a huge amphora are displayed leaning on a medieval cannon shell.

The main entrance to the old castle, with bits of carved marble and a row of cannon found on the premises.

lennium before Christ, had been laboriously dredged up from 90 feet of water in the eastern Mediterranean, from the oldest known shipwreck in the world. They came from a little Phoenician coastal trader, only 10 feet wide and 30 feet long, which sank off Cape Gelidonya, in south Turkey, more than three thousand years ago.

The Cape Gelidonya ship, as it is called today, is destined to loom as large and as romantically in the annals of underwater archaeology as the sinking of the *Titanic* does in the more recent annals of great ocean liners. It upset all previous theories about just how long ago the seafaring Phoenicians (who lived along the Mediterranean coast in the area now called Syria) actually sailed the waters of the ancient world, and it led directly to the most startling advances in underwater-exploration equipment since the invention of the diving helmet more than a century ago.

Cape Gelidonya's ship was found, like Troy, by a dedicated amateur with guts and imagination and perseverance. The story began in 1953, when a Turkish trawler captain beating the island-strewn coast of southwestern Turkey hauled up in his trawl the bronze head of a woman. Trawler captains are not trained to recognize antiquities, and they normally resent all such net-fouling objects as natural enemies to be destroyed on the spot ("so they can't tear the nets again") or tossed back overboard with a curse. Undoubtedly this captain would have done so, except that one of his sailors made the suggestion first. The captain, outraged that a mere crewman could attempt to give directions, instantly countermanded the whole idea. They would *not* throw the head back into the sea, he said belligerently. They would throw it onto the beach and later cut it up for scrap.

They did throw the head onto the beach, but before they could get back to begin demolishing it, Turkish authorities found it and recognized it as a priceless Greek bronze casting of the head of Demeter, goddess of the fruitful earth. They paid the trawlermen $10 for the head, far less than it would have fetched even as scrap, and carried it off in triumph to the Izmir Archaeological Museum.

One of the people who read about the beautiful Demeter was an American journalist/photographer, sailor, skin diver, and

The beautiful bronze head of Demeter on the right was found by a trawlerman by accident in 1953, near Bodrum, in southwestern Turkey.

amateur archaeologist named Peter Throckmorton. He was in Turkey at the time, so he went off to Izmir to see the head and inquire about the location of the wreck from which it had come. In Izmir he made friends with a Turkish diver/photographer named Mustafa Kapkin, and the two of them tried to find the trawler captain who had found the Demeter. The captain was nowhere around. So Throckmorton and Mustafa took to hanging around the seaport haunts of trawlermen and sponge divers, talking shop. The sponge divers were lugubrious. Plastic sponges, they said, were putting them out of business, and besides, there was so much "junk" littering the sea bottom that it was difficult to work. It was especially bad at a place called Yassi Ada ("flat island"), only 15 miles from Bodrum. There the sea bottom was littered with jars and odd lumps—hundreds of them, especially in two heaps lying on the bottom in about 120 feet of water.

Throckmorton and Mustafa then went to Bodrum and got acquainted with a sponge-boat captain who agreed to take them out to see Yassi Ada, to a place where they could dive near it. When they set forth, Throckmorton noticed that the Turkish divers were using lead weights which were unmistakably of Roman origin. The ancient Romans had used wooden anchors, but protected them and weighted them with lead, and the lead the sponge divers were using had come from these old anchor stocks. The ship's water tank, in addition, was a Roman amphora lashed to the mast. When Throckmorton inquired about the lead and the amphora, the captain shrugged and said they just picked up "this stuff" from the bottom of the sea. Both were of better quality, and lasted longer, than modern lead and modern water jars, he explained.

In that first series of dives around Yassi Ada, in 1958, Throckmorton located and charted for himself the wrecks of more than fifteen ships, dating from the third century B.C. to very recent times. He realized that the whole area was a gold mine for the underwater archaeologist, and he lingered in Bodrum. In the evenings, he spent hour after hour talking with sponge men. What happened next has been chattily and excitingly told by Peter Throckmorton himself in a book called *Lost Ships*, published by Atlantic–Little, Brown in 1963.

Mr. Throckmorton's book deserves to be read—but briefly, what happened was that he heard, from his new friends, about a hoard of "bronzes" heaped up on the bottom of the sea. Turkish divers had brought up bronze propellers, bits of copper, knife blades, and a hatchet to sell as scrap, and one reported that the stuff really wasn't much good because "I took a piece of it home and it broke when the children played with it."

One evening the talk turned to the uses of dynamite on the sea bottom to break loose "a mass of stuff grown flat to the bottom." What kind of stuff? Throckmorton asked, and his friend said big, flat bronze ingots—heavy, glued together in a mass, and badly corroded.

At this moment, amateur archaeologist Throckmorton began to turn into the professional that he is today. He rushed back to his room to consult what he calls his "packing box library," and in it he found a book with a reproduction of an Egyptian tomb painting from Thebes that showed just such strange flat ingots. In the illustration, the ingots were being presented as tribute to a rather bored-looking Egyptian official, and Throckmorton thought they resembled "giant flat dog biscuits." Nevertheless, he was so excited that he made a very rash offer: if his Turkish friend who had found the bronzes and who wanted to dynamite them would take him to the site, he would guarantee him double the going price for salvage. Maybe, Throckmorton told him, he might want to salvage the bronzes himself, but he would pay double. The deal was made, but it was another year before Throckmorton could scrounge enough money and a boat to make the almost 200-mile trip from Bodrum around the southern Turkish coast to the mysterious site which turned out to be Cape Gelidonya.

There, at the foot of a slope in the sea bed, and wedged in a natural amphitheater of rock with what appeared to be a huge boulder at one end of it, lay the wreck of a ship. And there, just as his friend had said, was a heap of odd-shaped ingots, dozens of them, locked solidly together by the centuries and by the undersea accretions. Fighting off all suggestions of dynamite, Throckmorton and the little crew managed, with enormous effort and a stout crowbar, to pry up one ingot and haul it triumphantly to shore. Under it was another surprise: bits of such highly perishable items as wood and even the remnants of a rope basket made from reeds and grasses twisted together by hand. Their preservation was a miracle of chemical reaction and the position of the wreck. Copper salts released by the corrosion of the ingots themselves had mixed with the drifting sands to form a mushy cushion which had maintained the integrity of the wood and the rope.

Dazzled by his find but nearly bankrupt from the expense of finding it, Throckmorton went back to the United States and reported everything to University of Pennsylvania archaeologists. He told them of the Cape Gelidonya wreck, of the jar-strewn seas around Yassi Ada, and of his own priceless contacts with those indefatigable explorers of the depths, the sponge fishermen. The latter, while friendly enough fellows, don't see the point of hauling up "junk" from the sea bottom unless they do it themselves, for salvage. By taking the time to explain and by winning their friendship, Throckmorton finally made allies—at least temporarily—of the men who know where the wrecks lie, and of the scientists who want to find them and explore them for knowledge.

By June, 1960, an expedition from the university, with support from the National Geographic Society, was back at Cape Gelidonya. It set up a camp on the forbidding beach and anchored an old fishing boat over the wreck so that divers could work. Head of the expedition was Pennsylvania University's Dr. George F. Bass, an experienced land archaeologist who was then in his midtwenties and who had never been more than 10 feet under water in his life. He had gotten acquainted with the rudiments of diving gear at the YMCA in Philadelphia; now, aided by the experienced Throckmorton and by diver/scientist Frederic Dumas, he learned fast.

Just as in the United States space program there developed an ideological conflict between the pure pilots and the scientist/astronauts, so in this underwater "dig" there was a basic difference of opinion between the divers and the archaeologists. Dr. Bass, Dumas, and Throckmorton all agreed that no material should be moved from the ocean floor until the entire area of the wreck had been accurately measured, charted, mapped, and photographed. Only then could they begin to remove the cargo. Just as a potsherd on land reveals little if the archaeologist doesn't know precisely where it was found, and at what level, and in what relationship to other artifacts, so a bit of ingot or a piece of an anchor chain from a shipwreck becomes little more than a curiosity if it is not related to all the other elements of cargo and construction. While the scientists measured, the divers fretted. Their time on the bottom was severely limited, and they wanted to get on with raising all the objects they could find. Dr. Bass, Throckmorton was later to write, drove the divers crazy. "[He] often spent his entire dive contemplating a bit of rotten wood, deciding what to do with it, while the experienced divers wondered how long it would be before he lost his mind completely."

The summer of 1960 turned out to be a very long one indeed. It was excruciatingly hot; rocks fell into the beach campsite from the surrounding hills; the expedition was plagued by galloping indigestion from imperfect hygienic arrangements; tempers grew short; the divers were visited by unmarked Turkish sailing vessels which cruised ominously near them because there were rumors that the Americans had "found a treasure in gold." Still, by September the expedition could be called a success. It succeeded in mapping the entire area of the wreckage and in recovering 95 per cent of the ancient ship's cargo. An amazingly vivid picture emerged from the waters. The little ship had set forth from the island of Cyprus, between 1300 and 1200 B.C., on a routine business trip up the now-Turkish coast. She carried about forty of the heavy "oxhide" ingots, more than half of which bore foundry marks written in a still-undeciphered Cypro-Minoan writing. (The Minoans in this era had a flourishing culture on the island of Crete.) She carried hundreds of bronze tools, weapons, household utensils, and even a device called a "swage block," which is an iron block containing holes and grooves of various sizes. It was used for heading bolts, and for shaping objects that are difficult to work on an anvil. The swage block, which is still in use today, thus turns out to be an invention more than three thousand years old. From all the interior evidence of cargo and of tools, the archaeologists have guessed that the ill-fated little ship must have been either owned or chartered by a traveling tinker of Phoenician times, a mender and manufacturer of tools and pots and pans and weapons, who plied his highly skilled trade from "door to door" along the ancient coast line.

He left no record of his name, but he left some very human and intimate traces in the wreckage. Divers found the terra-cotta lamp he used in his cabin, the only lamp on board, and they found a beautiful little carved cylinder seal of hard black stone that was five hundred years older than the ship itself and must have been one of his most prized possessions. In the congealed lump that turned out to be remnants of the cabin itself, the archaeologists found what remained of his last meal—a few olive pits, and the small bones of either a fish or a bird.

Shipwrecks have an irresistible fascination for human beings. Who cannot remember, in details as vivid as if one had, oneself, heard the wind and the waves, the cries of alarm and the screech of a lifeboat's oarlocks, the stories of the wreck of the British naval vessel *Nautilus* in the Aegean Sea in 1807, the death of the great liner *Titanic* in 1912, the dramatic sinking of the modern Italian passenger ship *Andrea Doria* in 1956?

Shipwrecks uniquely combine the thrill of adventure, the shiver of the unknown, the romance of the sea, and the mesmerizing terror of sudden disaster. For the archaeologist they mean even more: each one of them is a kind of time capsule, a sealed and complete record of its moment in history and in the development of the arts of shipbuilding and navigation. Under the sea, beneath waving marine plants or drifting sand, are a million clues to the life of the ancient world. All the seas are fascinating, but for the archaeologist none can compare with the placid-looking but often treacherous Mediterranean. It was here, thousands of years ago, that man first ventured out onto the water, cautiously, on logs or rafts, passionately invoking his gods for protection. It was here the first shipwreck must have occurred, and for all those thousands of years man has continued to have shipwrecks. Estimates of the number of ships at the bottom of the Mediterranean, from Phoenician and Egyptian times until today, vary from 5,000 to 100,000. Each, if it could be found, could speak volumes of how its crew lived, the utensils they used, the cargo they carried. To know the trade routes and cargoes of seafaring nations before the dawn of Christianity would be to learn much. The ships that made it safely to harbor will never be seen again. The unfortunate ones that didn't make it could speak, now, for their fellows. For all the wonders of land archaeology, one whole watery chapter is missing. Most land ruins have been battered by time and marching armies, by treasure hunters and wall builders. But under the sea, the record is relatively undisturbed. It is today in enormous danger from the marauding forays of skin divers looking for "treasure" and salvage divers looking for "junk," but if a wreck can be found undisturbed it is of immense value to archaeology.

For centuries the only men who knew the bottom of the Mediterranean were the sponge fishermen. Until the invention of the first protective diving dress about 1840, these stout fellows leaped nude into the water and managed brief, incredible dives down to 200 feet to snatch their living from the rocks in the form of sponges. Now and again one of them came upon a strange bronze object on the bottom, or a bit of sculptured stone, but by and large he ignored them. Who would bother with a piece of junk when there were sponges to be had?

Sponge divers were often hired to perform certain specific salvage—rescuing anchor stocks when the chain broke, fishing up objects that had fallen overboard, and the like. They performed their first archaeological service in 1802 by rescuing part of the famous "Elgin Marbles" which Britain's Lord Elgin had acquired from the Acropolis in Athens (Chapter 7). Seventeen cases of antiquities were on board the brig *Mentor* when she was caught in a gale in September, 1802, and sank in 60 feet of water near a harbor on the Greek island of Kytherea. Desperate, Lord Elgin sent for sponge divers to salvage his cargo, and although they thought the Englishman insane, the divers managed to haul all of the crates' contents up onto the beach. They lay there throughout the winter, covered with seaweed for protection, until another ship came out from England to take the precious marbles to London and to the British Museum.

In 1900 another group of Greek sponge divers performed the

In the dark alleys of Bodrum one can buy sponges (center) and ancient amphorae brought up from the sea.

world's first true marine archaeology, completely by accident. They scared themselves half to death in the process. They had anchored routinely off the rocky coast of the island of Antikythera, and an experienced diver put on his suit and his helmet and went casually over the side, gripping the safety rope while crewmen worked a hand pump to feed him air and a ship's boy kept his eyes on an hourglass to measure the time down below. This diver suddenly shot back to the surface before his time was up. Even through the murky, distorting glass of his primitive helmet, the crewmen could see that he was agitated. Hurriedly they got his helmet off, handed him a cigarette, tried to question him, while he mumbled, "Holy Virgin" over and over again to himself. He was trembling and babbled about "Horses, women, naked women . . . people, like a city, with men, and horses . . ." He could say no more.

The sponge captain, thinking that his best diver had suddenly gone mad, put on the diving gear himself and went below. He too came back up in a terrible hurry; but he had tied his safety line around a protruding *something* down there in the murky water, and he urged the sailors to haul it up. They tugged and struggled, and up came a greenish metal human hand, life size. The sponge divers had never seen or heard of such a thing, but the captain thought that it must be a shipwreck, a shipwreck of a kind he had never before encountered.

The sponge boat stayed there for several days, while divers battered loose and brought to the surface a whole heap of sculptured heads, arms, legs. The finds were so sensational that the Greek government intervened, commandeered the sponge fishers, and launched a salvage operation of its own. The ship turned out to have been Roman, probably carrying artistic cargo from ancient Greece to the wealthy capital of the Roman Empire, Rome itself.

It is a startling fact that almost half of the known Greek bronzes in the world today have been found this way—by accident, by fishermen. A rare Phoenician bronze statute of the god Melkarth came up in the nets of a Sicilian fishing boat a dozen years ago; the Demeter in the Izmir museum, as we know, was found by a trawlerman. A stunning Greek bronze head of a Negro boy, now in the Bodrum, Turkey, museum, was found by sponge fishers in 1963.

This random, hit-or-miss system has long troubled archaeologists, but there was little they could do about it. The learned professors couldn't dive, and the divers weren't interested in learned professors even if they had ever met any. In the explosion of scientific and technical knowledge that came at the end of World War II, however, techniques and machines have been developed to make orderly searches under the water entirely possible, even if never easy. In the span of less than twenty years, underwater archaeology has become the most rapidly developing branch of the whole engaging profession, and one of the most exciting. It began in Italy and in France, where the Italian professor Nino Lamboglia and the French scientist/divers Jacques-Yves Cousteau and Philippe Taillez worked in the early '50s at trying to raise submerged ancient wrecks. Three times they failed, but three times they managed to raise enormous amounts of cargo for study.

In 1958, Professor Lamboglia conducted the world's first truly *archaeological* exploration under water on what has become known as the "Sparghi ship," off the north coast of the island of Sardinia. The Sparghi ship was a little Roman cargo vessel which struck a rock in the dangerous Corsara Shallows sometime between 120 and 100 B.C. and sank with its full load of amphorae. Professor Lamboglia was determined to excavate the wreck under water exactly as good excavators do on land: by measuring the precise dimensions of the ship and its cargo, photographing it, drawing each detail minutely, and then, only then, bringing up the cargo layer by layer. He devised an ingenious tape webbing divided into squares 2 yards by 2 yards each, and divers carried it below, fitted it over the wreck, and staked it down. Then they carefully sketched and photographed each square, moved a layer of jars, and began the process over again. They used a giant underwater vacuum cleaner to remove sand so that they wouldn't damage the more deeply buried jars. In the end they had the clearest, most useful concept ever obtained as to the construction of an ancient ship, the loading of its cargo, and the life aboard. The system was far from perfect, but it was a giant step.

Another Greek bronze, the head of a Negro boy, was found by sponge fishermen in 1963. The small photograph at right shows how the ancient bronze looked when it was fished out of the sea.

The next giant step came in 1960 with full exploration of the Cape Gelidonya wreck, and it was followed by a 1961 dig in which the veterans of Gelidonya went back to the island of Yassi Ada to work on one of the fifteen wrecks Throckmorton had found there in 1958. This time they chose a Byzantine merchant ship which had struck a reef just off the island on a day in about A.D. 740 and sunk, with cargo and all hands, into 115 feet of water. When work began, the only visible parts of the old ship were six iron anchors at the bow, a few round amphorae which stuck out of the sand, and a tumbled heap of roof tiles and cooking pots where the ship's galley had been.

This time the archaeologists improved upon Lamboglia's grid by setting up a complicated and funny-looking gadget which came to be known as "Bass's bedsprings." It too was a grid, but it was made of more rigid metal bars with wire cross-sectioning. It could be set up over the wreckage and adjusted for height so that more accurate measurements could be taken. It also had the advantage of remaining stable under water. Underwater photography had proved useful on both the Sparghi ship and the Cape Gelidonya ship, but this time the diggers opted for cameras mounted on towers on top of the bedsprings. The cameras could be moved more precisely, and there was less possibility of diver disorientation in photographing the vestiges of the shipwreck.

There seems to be no end to the ingenuity of the underwater archaeologists. When the Pennsylvania group first encountered the problem of prying loose those heavy bronze ingots at Cape Gelidonya, Throckmorton had the inspiration of finding a hydraulic automobile jack, digging a hole to seat it well, and then jacking up the whole ingot pile until it came loose. That worked. In 1961 at Yassi Ada they used the same technique to pry loose and raise the ancient cannon.

When they came upon fragments of the original ship's timbers in the Yassi Ada wreck, but found them so fragile that they floated away if disturbed by any movement in the water, George Bass bought two thousand stainless steel bicycle spokes and used them like giant thumbtacks to hold the rotting timbers in place long enough for divers to sketch them, meticulously.

Whereas Lamboglia's men had floated amphorae to the surface

with plastic balloons or hoisted them in a box lift, the divers of the Yassi Ada expedition found a simpler way: they simply removed the air hoses from their own mouths for a moment and thrust them into the mouths of the jars. Then when they released the jars they shot upward like corks to bob on the surface, where crewmen could snag them and take them aboard the expedition boat.

They even solved the problem of decompression boredom. Divers working at 115 feet, as at Yassi Ada, must pause at least twice on the way back up to decompress and avoid the bends. The custom was to pause at a depth of 20 feet for three minutes, at 10 feet for eighteen minutes. These can seem very long minutes indeed, but the ingenious divers found a simple solution: they read books. In the clear water off the island, the visibility was excellent, and a paperback, they discovered, could be read easily under water. It wasn't much good afterward on dry land, but no matter. They simply hung a handy pailful of paperbacks 10 feet down and, like commuters, browsed through the books while waiting. George Bass once confided to a friend that he had read all of Norman Mailer's *The Deer Park* under water.

By the end of 1963, the Yassi Ada "dig" had yielded the largest and most accurately dated cache of Byzantine pottery ever found. Out of the wreckage came, in addition to pottery, eleven anchors, a collection of gold and copper coins, ax blades, adzes, hammers, nails, plates and goblets, and two bronze hand-held weighing scales almost identical to those used by street merchants all around the rim of the Mediterranean today. A scale of this type has a long arm stretching out at the side, along which counterbalancing weights are moved in very much the same fashion as one moves the weight across an arm on the weighing scale at the doctor's office. One of the two Byzantine scales, which is now in the Bodrum museum in that Crusader castle, has an arm almost 5 feet long. Inscribed on it in Byzantine Greek is the name of the long-dead captain: "George the Elder, senior sea officer."

From Cape Gelidonya in 1960 until the present writing, the expeditions of George Bass and the University of Pennsylvania have been an experimental laboratory for the study of advanced techniques in underwater archaeology. They still sometimes use the underwater vacuum cleaner designed by Cousteau and used by Lamboglia, but the tape grids and the "bedsprings" have given way to an adaption of the sophisticated method of aerial and even lunar mapping photography. This method, in simplest terms, involves an aircraft or a spacecraft flying over a specific area to be mapped. While it flies, automatic cameras take a series of photographs at calculated intervals. The cameras are set to take pictures which accurately overlap one another, so that when put through the lens of a three-dimensional stereo viewer they permit experts to make accurate readings of distance and depth.

In the relatively small-scale scope of underwater photography of shipwrecks, there is no need for either spacecraft or airplanes, but there is great need for accurate stereophotographs. The Yassi Ada diggers solved the problem by suspending a metal bar from two weighted balloons, 25 feet above the wreck. On the bar they hung a standard Rollei-Marine underwater camera with a leveling device. The divers then made the camera "fly" by moving it along the bar at calculated intervals so that one photo would overlap another. The system worked: when the stereo pairs were examined with a Zeiss Stereoscope, they gave a three-dimensional perspective which could be measured. The refraction of light in the water itself caused some distortion, however, and the scientists went back to their famous drawing board to devise corrective lenses. Even with its defects, this "Model T" system of underwater photogrammetry proved that two or three divers could do in a few days what fifteen divers had done in nearly two months in the first season at Yassi Ada.

As every experimenter knows, the solution of one problem often does little more than create a dozen new problems. While the most urgent needs of underwater measurement and salvage were being met and solved, the problem of preservation loomed larger. Some Phoenician glass beads found in the wreck of the Cape Gelidonya ship seemed hard and strong under water, but after only a few days on land they blew up into tiny particles of dust. Italian archaeologists have found ancient Roman iron in the seas of their coast and hauled it laboriously ashore only to watch it turn to greenish mush in the air. Often the "lumps" brought up from an underwater dig are in fact nothing but casts of the object that once lay within. The metal once inside has corroded away and left only a blackened, sandy mold which formed around it during the centuries. Such "lumps" can be used, however: archaeologists saw them carefully in half to reveal a perfect cast of the original object. At first they used plaster in these casts, but the Pennsylvania researchers have discovered that rubber compounds work better.

Wood is one of the most delicate materials to handle after long submersion, and yet it is one of the most vital. The ancient ships were without exception made of wood, and it is the dream of all underwater excavators to someday raise a sunken ship and reconstruct it on land. Wood can look almost fresh, and very sturdy, under water, and it can have survived for two thousand, three thousand years. Yet once on land it will fall apart, disintegrate into dust, if it is not properly treated. To make matters worse, the rate of decay of the wood, and its tolerance for fresh air again, depends upon whether it lay in fresh water or in salt water; upon whether the water was warm or cold; upon the specific depth at which the wood lay.

In 1963 the Pennsylvania expedition was grappling with the crucial problem of wood. Having cleared the Byzantine wreck at Yassi Ada of all its cargo, and having carefully drawn a plan of its wooden remains under the sea, the archaeologists tried to move the planking and the ribs to shore. George Bass explained this operation, graphically, in a 1964 report to *Anatolian Studies*, the Journal of the British Institute of Archaeology at Ankara: "It was found that it was nearly impossible to haul wood to the surface in open baskets, no matter how slowly, without damaging it. A 15 meters long [almost 50 feet] wire basket, long enough to contain the largest preserved timbers, was made, therefore, with six handles. Six divers, wearing shoes rather than fins, placed timbers into this basket, and walked with it to a beach on Yassi Ada about 100 meters away and 40 meters higher on the slope. After each piece of wood was redrawn in detail, it was soaked in baths of fresh water for several months awaiting treatment in polyethylene glycol."

It may be years before the archaeologists, and their scientific allies the chemists, decipher the mysterious chemical changes that occur in materials under water, and discover what to do to preserve the artifacts so carefully, painstakingly, expensively resurrected.

In the field of simple undersea exploration, the archaeologists and technicians are making gigantic strides. In the past ten years a whole fleet of sounding devices, undersea cameras, magnetometers, closed-circuit television systems, and strange-looking submarines has been developed to widen the search for that older, long-lost fleet down below. George Bass spent most of one summer towing an underwater television camera behind a boat and sitting with his eyes glued to the screen looking for ancient wrecks. He reported later that "all I saw was murk." He tried the Tow-Vane, a small bathysphere which can be towed under water by a surface craft to photograph the ocean bottom on closed-circuit TV. He even tried a proton magnetometer, a by-product of basic research in nuclear physics. This device measures magnetic changes and variations in materials it cannot see, and has been used successfully in land archaeology to locate buried masonry and the traces of tombs and lost cities. All these devices helped, but none was perfect.

In 1967 the Pennslyvania expedition tried two of them in combination, and achieved a moment of glorious success. It was back again at Yassi Ada, this time searching for the wreck of the ship from which that Turkish sponge fisherman had taken the Greek bronze head of a Negro boy in 1963. If there was one bronze head, Bass thought, there might be more. Perhaps there would be marble statues as well. He and his fellow archaeologists had guessed that the ship must have been Roman, and that it had sunk about two thousand years ago. But where to look, and at what depth, in the vast sea bed around the island?

To begin the search, they brought out a device called the sonar detector. This is an electronic instrument which emits sound waves at frequencies of 5,000 to 20,000 cycles per second, traveling at the rate of 1,600 yards per second. When the sound waves strike an object, they are reflected back again. Receiving instruments record this "bounce" and calculate in milliseconds the time it took for the sound wave to go out, hit something, and come back. The information is recorded in the form of a graph, which indicates how far away the sound-reflecting object lies, and at what depth. The sonar detector at Yassi Ada was mounted on wheels, lowered into the sea near the presumed site of the Roman wreck, and then towed across the bottom at the end of a cable attached to a trawler. Bass and his crew waited, anxiously, on board the trawler. Suddenly, before their eyes, the receiver graph marked five distinct bumps or protuberances on the ocean floor. There was something down there.

At this point the story begins to sound like science fiction. The trawler dropped a buoy to mark the site of the bumps, and the archaeologists crawled into a midget submarine called the *Asherah*. The *Asherah*, named for a Phoenician goddess of the sea, was designed and built specifically for the University of Pennsylvania by the Electric Boat Division of General Dynamics. She can make only 2.5 knots and she is only 17 feet long, but she can operate at depths up to 600 feet while carrying detection gear, automatic stereo cameras, closed-circuit television, and two very excited archaeologists. In half an hour this new goddess *Asherah* can take as many photographs as a dozen divers can take in a month. She can also stay down infinitely longer than divers can— ten hours—and she doesn't need to remember to take along a paperback, because she can surface quickly with no need to stop and decompress.

On this exciting day in the summer of 1967, *Asherah*, who had dived before on archaeological business, went down 300 feet, picked out the buoy line, went for it, and hit the jackpot. There on the sea bottom was a bumpy heap of sand in the outline of a ship. There were some terra-cotta tiles which Dr. Bass surmised had once been on the roof of the ship's galley, and there was a jumbled heap nearby which showed the ship's big water jar and other bits of pottery.

It would have been much more appropriate to the romantic mind, of course, if this seagoing goddess *Asherah* had been used to find that ship of her own era, the Phoenician trader off Cape Gelidonya, but this day was triumph enough.

Legend, for there is legend even under water, says that the Macedonian king Alexander the Great, conqueror of most of the

The archaeological submarine Asherah *is seen in action under water. Strong lights and cameras can be rigged in the forward portholes, and the rack on the nose of the ship can be used to mount any other equipment—lights, still and TV cameras, sonar detectors, and so on.*

known world in the third century B.C., once decided to see what lay below and ordered a great glass barrel made for himself. In it he put lamps, and he had himself lowered on ropes to great depths in the very sea which *Asherah* explored. This is an unbelievable tale, because even had it been possible to make a glass barrel strong enough to go to "great depths," the lamps inside would quickly have consumed the oxygen in the barrel and suffocated the king. Yet as late as the 13th century of the Christian Era there were written accounts of this marvelous voyage, saying that Alexander saw "many fish that had the form of beasts that live on land and walk on legs . . . and many other wonders that were unbelievable."

We may well doubt the descent of Alexander the Great under the waters, but we can never doubt as much as Alexander himself would have doubted had he heard of the fantastic voyage of the *Asherah*. In the wonderful world of archaeology, we are all part of the legend.

14

LEGENDS COME ALIVE

Once upon a time, if we are to believe the legends that we hear, there was a king called Croesus who was so wealthy that for 2,500 years people have continued to say, of anyone with more money than he knows how to spend, that he is "rich as Croesus."

Ancient historians said that Croesus ruled the kingdom of Lydia about 550 B.C. and that he had a river literally full of gold running through his capital city. The river was called the Pactolus, and it still exists, meandering among some jagged red cliffs and pinnacles in western Turkey only 50 miles inland from Izmir. Today the Pactolus is full of mud, small children, and archaeologists. Was it ever full of gold, and where did the gold come from? There is a legend that tells about that too. There was another king, called Midas, who ruled a country called Phrygia about 150 miles farther east into Turkey. Midas lived before Croesus, and as a king in a pre-Christian world he was much under the influence of the pagan Greek gods—Apollo, Dionysus, Artemis, and all the rest. Kings, gods, and mortals were on much closer terms in those days than they are today, and it happened, according to the legend, that Midas was entertaining one of the gods at a dinner one night. In the enthusiasm of good-fellowship,

The once-golden river of Croesus, the Pactolus, now is a favorite play-ground for neighborhood children.

the god offered to grant King Midas one wish—any wish he wanted. The foolish king wished that everything he touched would be turned to gold, and the wish was granted. Delightedly Midas touched drinking cups, dishes, chairs, and they turned to gold. But then he got hungry, and as he touched his food it turned to gold. So did his water and his wine, and presumably even his wife and his children. Dismayed, he implored the god Dionysus to take away what had become a curse. Dionysus told him the only way to cancel the wish was to go and bathe in the River Pactolus. From the moment of that bath, the Pactolus ran bank to bank with gold flakes washed from Midas.

It is a recorded fact that one way the ancients used to remove gold flakes from rivers was to put sheepskins on the riverbed to snare the flakes in the white wool, and from this practice may have come still another legend, that of the "golden fleece," in search of which Jason and his Argonauts sailed the seas.

Everybody loves a legend, and archaeologists, far from being cold-eyed, hardhearted scientists, love legends perhaps more than most. They use legends, as Schliemann used the *Iliad*, as a kind of folklore gospel, a set of intriguing clues in the continuing search to put back together the shattered jigsaw puzzle that is the long story of mankind. All over modern Turkey the search for the legend goes on.

One of the most avid search groups sets out each year from the University Museum of the University of Pennsylvania. More than twenty years ago the university's Dr. Rodney Young decided to look for Midas and for his capital city of Gordion. He chose a site southwest of Ankara, the present capital of Turkey, led to the spot by a conjunction of rivers—always a favorite location for the foundation of cities—and by traces of a great "royal road" which the Persians had built after they swept through this part of Anatolia. There was one big flat mound which might be the remains of the city of Gordion, and the plain around it was dotted with lesser mounds which could be the tombs of the kings of the Phrygians. In the years of digging, the low flat mounds yielded evidence of five distinct settlements, each with several subdivisions, dating from the third millennium B.C. to the time of the Phrygians, from 1200 to 700 B.C.; then the Persians; and finally the Greeks and the Galatians. Gates, city walls, the remains of palaces, all lay where they should logically have been if this were Gordion, and though Dr. Young says "no direct evidence, such as an inscription mentioning the name of Gordion, has been found on the site, it is generally agreed that the identification of our mound with ancient Gordion is correct."

With the city found, the search for Midas went on more intensively. Each year the expedition worked gingerly at the smaller mounds, learning their general construction, trying out the best methods for their excavations. By 1956 they were ready to explore the most fascinating· mound of all, a towering 175-foot tumulus fit for a king. "Since the mound is a monument in itself, it seemed undesirable to destroy it by digging down from the top," said Dr. Young. This method certainly would have demolished it, because the Phrygian kings never permitted themselves to be buried in a chamber in the precise center of the tumulus. That would have made it far too easy for the treasure hunters and grave robbers of their own era to plunder their tombs. To search for the small burial chamber in the huge mound, then, Dr. Young brought in a light oil-drilling rig and "felt around" inside the tumulus with it. After about a hundred borings, he thought they had located the exact position and the size of the heap of stones that the Phrygians usually piled up over the burial vault itself. Now they could go straight down from the top, digging a sort of well to get to the tomb, or they could tunnel in from the bottom of the mound. They decided upon a tunnel, and imported a crew of professional miners to do the work. For twenty-five days the miners toiled away, digging out a tunnel more than 220 feet long. At the end they ran into a stone wall, which everyone excitedly thought must be the wall of the tomb. The miners hacked an opening into the wall, and instantly a stream of small gravel-like stones poured out. The stream became a river, and within minutes the tunnel was completely blocked.

Patiently, the workmen carried out the stones, but as fast as they carried them out, another river of rock inundated them. A Turkish workman still at the site recalls that "it went on for what seemed like a week. We thought we had found the fount of all the gravel on earth. It was as if we were to spend our lives there, like emptying the ocean with a sieve."

At the end of the week, however, they could peer into the hole in the wall and see heavy rough-cut wooden walls made of juniper 2 feet thick. Elated, the workmen bored an auger hole in the wood—and got another shower of pebbles. In his official report to the University of Pennsylvania in the autumn of 1958, Dr. Young described vividly what happened next: "There was nothing to do but cut a window through the wall big enough to show what lay within. As the auger had predicted, the window showed only more stone rubble. This time, however, we were not held long in suspense. After only about an hour enough rubble had been taken out to reveal the face of a second wooden wall, here made of nicely squared and fitted timbers rather than rough logs. The auger was at hand and bored through the wood without encountering stone at the other side. It was now certain that the tomb was intact and the roof unbroken. A small window was cut through the inner wall, big enough to insert only the head and one arm with a flashlight. The staff took turns in looking in; the tomb was large, the atmosphere dense, the flashlight weak. Among the wonders thus seen were a chariot, and a stuffed alligator!"

It was a rare find indeed, because virtually no royal tombs are found intact today. Inside the burial chamber, about 20 feet by 16 feet, was a great four-poster bed, and on it the skeleton of a man more than sixty years old when he died, a small man about 5 feet 2 inches tall. He wore a leather skirt with bronze studs and a long-sleeved shirt fastened with the bronze safety pins. Interred with him were the ordinary effects of the king's household: nine tables, two inlaid wooden screens, three bronze cooking caldrons on iron-ring stands. Each caldron was piled high with black-polished eating and cooking ware, in some of which were still remains of the food buried with the monarch. His jewelry, 145 bronze pieces wrapped in a linen cloth, had once been placed on a table beside the bed, but the table had collapsed and the jewelry lay scattered on the floor of the tomb. There were no weapons buried with him, and no precious jewelry or gold and silver objects. The chariot seen by the excited archaeologists in the "dense atmosphere" with a "weak flashlight" turned out to be an optical illusion caused by the collapse of wooden tables and tumbled caldrons. The stuffed alligator (or crocodile) must have been a gift to His Anonymous Highness from a friend in Egypt.

This gift, the wealth of objects, the size of the tomb, and the enormous care with which it had been built certainly indicated royalty. As they slowly and carefully finished the excavation, Dr. Young and his group figured out how the long-ago Phrygians constructed the elaborate tomb. First they laid out the general area and piled porous blocks of stone to make outer walls. Inside these walls, the tomb area itself was built carefully of two sets of wooden walls. Heaps of stone rubble were piled between the two wooden walls and then between the outer wooden one and the stone one. The entire structure, except for the roof, was finished up to roof level, and the much larger tumulus itself was begun around the outside. When the king died, his body and household effects were lowered inside, and then the roof was added. On the top of the roof went layer on layer of stones, and over this, clay. Gradually the rest of the enveloping, enormous tumulus was built up. The clay of this particular tumulus must have been damp when it was laid down, Dr. Young believes, because when he and his men pulled out the stones that covered the tomb roof there remained a hard dome of clay in which the outlines of the stone packing were still completely visible.

Though some Turkish archaeologists believe that the great tumulus was the tomb of King Midas, Dr. Young does not. He has dated it, from the pottery and other objects inside, to about 743 B.C., which is too early for Midas. Further, Dr. Young believes it unlikely that any tomb could have been constructed with such care, and furnished so lavishly, at the time Midas died. He is supposed to have been killed, suddenly and violently, by invading Cimmerians, and invaders seldom gave survivors time to take care of the king so meticulously. Perhaps, says Young, this king is one of a series of kings named Gordios for whom the city of Gordion was named in the first place.

Gordios takes us back to the legends again. The first Gordios was a mere Phrygian laborer who all unwittingly walked through the city gate one day and found himself proclaimed king. This

was because an oracle, who was a spokesman for one of the powerful gods, had said that whoever first walked through the gate after
a certain hour would be made ruler of the city. Dazed by his good
fortune, the new King Gordios made his thanks to the great god
Zeus, and then he went even further. He offered Zeus a splendid
chariot, and he tied the chariot's yoke and shaft together with
such a complicated knot that it was believed no mortal could ever
untie it. At this point the oracle spoke up again and announced
that anyone who could untie the "Gordian knot" would rule all
Asia. Nobody could, until along came Alexander the Great on his
way to conquering the known world. Legend says he looked the
knot over carefully and decided that no mere rope should daunt
his ambitions. So he whipped out his sword and cut it smack in
two. Whether this seemed like cheating to the citizens of Gordion
is not a matter of record; but it probably wouldn't have altered
the outcome much, because Alexander had his army with him at
the time.

No trace of the "Gordian knot" has turned up in the ruins of
the ancient city; but there were representations of chariots on
shields and pottery and metal objects, and there was that big
wooden bed on which some unknown ancient king was laid out
2,700 years ago. There were also the nine wooden tables. The
tables were almost as fortunate a find as the knot would have
been, for it confirmed another legend. This was that the great
King Midas had made an offering of a plain wooden table to the
temple of the god Apollo in Delphi, Greece. Archaeologists have
long puzzled over this one, because it was far more customary for
kings to offer silver and gold to the gods, not wood. Yet here,
laid out lovingly in the tomb of an unknown king, were tables
just like the one Midas gave Apollo. If they were good enough
for a king, they were worthy to offer to a god.

Part of the archaeologists' concern over what had seemed a
most modest gift from Midas to Apollo was that expensive pres-
ents were usually required to curry favor with gods. All kings in
those days, especially in the Greek world, consulted the gods for
advice and assistance, and they expected to be answered by the
gods' spokesmen, called oracles. Oracles usually resided inside the

temples of gods, and they were never really seen except perhaps in the form of priests or priestesses who relayed their information to those who came asking.

The greatest oracle of the time lived in the Temple of Apollo at Delphi, in Greece. After this Delphic oracle, one of the next most important was associated with another temple of Apollo at Didyma, in southwestern Turkey. Didyma was never truly a city. It was just a temple, and its ruins stand today as probably the most impressive single ancient monument on the western Turkish coast: an unbelievably enormous structure of columns and monumental staircases and carved heads among the weeds. Some early writers say that an oracle existed at Didyma even before the temple did, and modern archaeologists have found inscriptions on the site dating back to 600 B.C.

One of the inscriptions seems to be the fragment of a response from this ancient oracle, and it is highly significant because it explains a great deal about how oracles worked. The request, couched in the respectful terms that oracles required, was in fact a rather crass one: the local residents wanted to know if it was all right to engage in the lucrative practice of piracy, plundering foreign ships in the coastal waters nearby. The oracle replied enigmatically, "It is right to do as your fathers did." Now, there is very little doubt that their fathers had engaged in piracy quite happily, so the supplicants were delighted with the reply, and the oracle's reputation was heightened. It had refrained from counseling crime; it had made a pious but very convenient statement. If challenged, the oracle could claim quite rightly that it did not counsel doing *everything* your fathers did. No doubt offerings to the oracle were lavish for some time thereafter.

Supplicants approaching the oracle at Didyma normally did so by boat, landing on the shore and walking down a Sacred Way toward the temple, there to present their gifts and their requests. No caller ever saw the oracle, of course; callers presented their questions and their offerings to one or more of a group of priests and prophets and attendants who had the right and the ability to relay them to the oracle. At Didyma the means of communication between the oracle and the people was female, a kind of high priestess who took her exceptional powers from a sacred spring

This giant head of Medusa was once set in the frieze of the Temple of Apollo at Didyma, where a great oracle lived.

The massive, handsome ruins of the temple at Didyma.

within the confines of the temple. She relayed the oracle's words in writing. Some other oracles gave their answers merely by nods or signs, or by a rustling of wind in the trees, but the Didyma oracle was highly literate: its answers came back in elegantly written hexameter verse.

A fourth-century writer says that the priestess in Didyma always held in her hand a staff "given by a certain god" and that she prepared herself for communication with the oracle by wetting her feet or the hem of her robe in the sacred spring, or by inhaling its vapors. Furthermore, she abstained from food for three days. It all must, as one modern observer has noted, "have put her in a receptive mood, to say the least."

Whole platoons of helpers, assistant prophets, and other functionaries found employment around these oracular shrines, and sometimes local rulers appointed themselves prophets. It is astonishing to realize that the oracles continued for centuries. They were wiped out only by invading barbarian armies and/or by the rise of Christianity. Yet they could not have survived so long had all their advice been wrong, or ill advised. A great deal of it was very obscure in language, of course, and sometimes misleading. Much of the oracular counsel was as vague and all-embracing as the advice proffered in daily horoscopes printed in today's newspapers. Added to this was the fact that a report of a successful prophecy or a stunning bit of advice would travel rapidly, even in the ancient world. This would enhance the oracle's reputation, while at the same time a hundred bad guesses would be forgotten. Yet amazing things did happen. There is, for example, the legend of the founding of the great city of Ephesus on the west coast of Turkey. The founding fathers asked an oracle where would be a good place for a city, and the oracle said, "Find a spot which a fish and a wild boar will point out." That's the sort of answer that wouldn't satisfy anyone today, but the supplicants patiently settled back to wait for some strange conjunction of a fish and a wild boar. Sure enough, one night some fishermen settled down on the beach to cook part of their day's catch in a flaming brazier. One fish flopped out, with a live coal stuck to its skin, and set fire to some wood shavings nearby which the men had cut to use as tinder. The flames spread quickly to a nearby thicket, and a wild boar that had been hiding in the thicket rushed out in alarm. The oracle's words had come true. The city of Ephesus was built on the spot, and until A.D. 400 an effigy of a wild boar stood beside the main street of the city. This legend could have been invented in reverse, of course—an effigy of a wild boar having been seen and explained by some fanciful resident in the form of the legend of the oracle.

Another clue to the success of oracles must lie in the extraordinary amount of incidental information that all the various priestesses and prophets and their assistants picked up from all the people who came to consult the oracle. Simple citizens asking to be advised on the site of a new city might also bring news of the destruction of their old city. If two powerful and neighboring kings turned up, one after the other, to consult the oracle about making war, it wouldn't take much intelligence on the part of the oracle's assistants to assume that there was going to be bloodshed in the vicinity. An oblique reply from the oracle might stop the war, or it might enable the oracle to influence the course of the battle by the advice it gave.

Such was actually the case in one of the most famous oracular pronouncements to have come down to us through the centuries. The rich King Croesus, feeling himself threatened by the Persians to the east of him, consulted the oracle at Delphi about the wisdom of his attacking the Persians before they attacked him. The oracle brooded about this awhile, then pronounced that if Croesus attacked Persia he would "destroy a great empire." Naturally, Croesus thought this meant he would destroy Persia, so he attacked. He was wrong. He lost the battle to Cyrus and the Persians, and it was his own empire that he destroyed. But the oracle had spoken the truth.

To track down the legend of Croesus, the archaeologists had first to find his capital city, the "Golden Sardis" of myth and folklore. Actually, the site had never been totally lost: it lay on the edge of a plain at the foot of the often snow-capped Tmolus Mountains, inland from the sea near Izmir. It is a strange landscape of reddish hills carved by the wind and rain into turrets and castles, precipices and gorges, grotesque caricatures of human faces or animals against the sky. So oddly sculpted are the natural hills that the visitor finds it hard to decide which is the ruin of the old acropolis and which just another red hill knocked about by earthquake, flood, and storm. Here and there enormous columns have lain on the ground for centuries, slowly being buried by the thunderous landslides that roar out of the mountains after torrential winter rains. So unstable is the whole terrain that diggers can find one piece of a Byzantine monument poking up through the cotton fields of today's peasants and another piece, only a few yards away, buried under 30 feet of earth.

Before World War I, an American expedition from Princeton University managed to free two of the columns of one of the largest Greek temples in the world, dedicated to Artemis. But then work stopped; it remained suspended until 1958, when a joint Harvard-Cornell group arrived at the site of Sardis determined to dig it all out once and for all. They found immense remains from Roman and Byzantine times, including a huge marble Roman *palestra*, or gymnasium; sections of the great "royal road" of the Persians; and one of the oldest and most enormous synagogues in the world. Patiently the diggers pieced together 70 per cent of the glorious mosaics that had once decorated the synagogue. Their excavations revealed astounding new evidence of a wave of urban planning almost two thousand years ago, when an earthquake destroyed the city and its Roman rulers rebuilt it with special attention to water, and baths, and fine roads in all directions.

Out on the plain about six miles north of Sardis proper, some members of the expedition began digging in what they thought might be a Bronze Age cemetery, and could hardly believe their eyes when they uncovered enormous jars with the remains of farmers buried inside. The jars were 5 or 6 feet tall, and they dated from between 2500 and 2200 B.C. There was only one corpse in each jar, and as they carefully lifted them out, the men remembered one more legend: Ali Baba and the forty thieves. According to this tale, the forty thieves hid in forty immense jars, and their larcenous plot was foiled only when Ali Baba's slave Morgiana poured boiling oil into the jars.

The jars made it clear that this site had been inhabited from

The ruins of the Temple of Artemis in Sardis stand against the strange wind-and-water-sculptured red hills of the Tmolus Mountains. The temple was built in 300 B.C., after Alexander the Great had converted the Lydian city of Croesus to the Greek way of life. On the peak in the background once stood the acropolis of the city.

2500 B.C. clear into the Byzantine period, somehow surviving sack by the Persian king Cyrus about 550 B.C., capture by Alexander the Great a couple of centuries later, occupation by Rome, and destruction by earthquake repeatedly. The long record seems to end in A.D. 615, the precise period in which the Persian King Khosrau II overran the peninsula and got all the way to Constantinople before he was stopped. Coins found buried in the ruins of Sardis stop at A.D. 615, and though there may have been straggling settlements at the site later, "Golden Sardis" was finished. The present Turkish village of Sart is, like Samsat off near Nemrud Dagh, a sad successor to the glories of long ago.

Coins have always helped archaeologists immeasurably because they are relatively indestructible, often clearly dated, and so small they get lost in the ruins and can be located only by the patience of a proper dig. They assume a special significance in Sardis, however, for it was the Lydians who invented coinage. For centuries men engaged in elaborate barter systems of cattle for grain, of oil for wine, of bars of metal for perfume and cloth. In the fifth century B.C., Herodotus, who is called "the father of history," said firmly that "the Lydians were the first of mankind to strike and use a coinage of gold and silver." This has proved to be a useful fact for the eager diggers of Sardis. Like all archaeologists, they are in constant need of more money to continue their work, and they often seek out wealthy private citizens as prospective donors. The Sardis diggers can explain their work quickly by saying,

Old Sardis as it is being reconstructed today is one of the most ambitious renovation projects in all Turkey. In the foreground are the remains of a huge synagogue.

"This was the city that invented money." It's the kind of statement calculated to impress wealthy prospective donors.

At first the coinmakers of Sardis used a gold-and-silver alloy called electrum and stamped each piece with the symbol of their city, a lion and a bull, as a guarantee of its value. For the first time, merchants could carry real currency in a handy skin bag, instead of hauling around caravan loads of produce or lugging lumps of heavy metal in their saddlebags. The chief source of Sardis' gold was undoubtedly deposits of almost pure metal in those weirdly carved mountains, metal washed out by the storms and carried rushing through the Pactolus River. The source of the silver is more obscure, but may have been the plain of Troy, off to the north. The electrum currency of Sardis made the city rich—but then merchants noticed that the actual gold content of the coins could vary from 5 to 20 per cent. This set off possibly the world's first currency crisis, and rather than see his nation's coins devalued in the market place, King Croesus decided to go to "bimetallic coinage," a system in which a number of silver pieces could add up to one gold coin. Herodotus clearly said that it was Croesus who decreed this more refined coinage, and he added slyly that its use made the Lydians the first traveling salesmen.

Lydian coinage was so well known throughout the ancient world, and so well documented by archaeologists at dozens of sites, that its existence was not in doubt. But was it Croesus who decreed it, and did Croesus truly exist?

For season after season the Harvard-Cornell group dug, and despite the wonders they turned up, they could find no remains of the Lydian Sardis of the king. His entire golden city, with its painted gables and its strong colors, had vanished without a trace. Archaeologists assumed that much of it had simply slid down into the riverbed and that the final damage was done by Byzantines, who rooted up all the remains of the Lydian city to build a colossal defense wall.

In the season of 1967, however, the expedition made an exciting discovery: an unmistakable shrine to the Lydian goddess Cybele, with her four sculptured lions still standing escort. This shrine could have dated from Croesus' time. Near it they came upon a tiny solid-gold earring. Expedition members delightedly photographed the earring and had it printed on post cards to send to friends and supporters—but that was all they found.

Then came the summer of 1968. A group of excavators went back to the site of the shrine of Cybele, near the Pactolus River, to scrape around some more. One of the workers was Andrew Ramage, an Englishman who went to Cambridge but who was then a graduate student in classical archaeology at Harvard. Ramage was on his hands and knees brushing carefully at a packed-clay floor near the shrine when suddenly he spotted some odd circular depressions in the clay. The edge of each depression was slightly tinged with a shiny, greenish slag which occurs only when elements have been exposed to extreme heat. Excitedly he kept on brushing and looking. Within a few days he found some three hundred of these little rings, or depressions, in layers super-imposed on top of one another. Each depression was from 6 to 12 inches in diameter and from 4 to 6 inches deep.

"I announced to everybody that we had found King Croesus' refinery," Ramage said later with a chuckle. "At first I touted the idea as a wild suggestion, a joke. But then we began to talk about it more seriously."

Actually four years earlier another archaeologist had seen one or two of the "rings" and had jumped to no conclusion whatever, so excavation director George M. A. Hanfmann of the Fogg Art Museum at Harvard was inclined to accept Ramage's remark as a joke. "We began to say, 'Wouldn't it be nice if this *were* a refinery?' " he recalls. "But we were joking. Then we began to wonder."

They began to wonder because lead slag turned up in the debris of the area. Slag, sometimes called cinder, is a by-product of the process of refining metal from ore, and its presence means somebody has been refining crude ore. Shortly after this discovery, Ramage and a colleague, sifting carefully through the slag and dirt, turned up several fragments of pure gold. Two weeks later, they uncovered four furnaces about 20 yards from the site of the gold flakes, and then they found the battered metal remains of the nozzles of bellows.

For all that the river ran with gold, Croesus would have needed more than its gold flakes to make enough currency for a kingdom.

This implied that he had to find a way to refine pure metal from ore. The remnants the archaeologists found turned out to be a simple refining system of a kind that was still in use until medieval times and in some areas even later.

It was actually two separate processes. In the first, workmen lined each little depression, which is called a "cupel," or refining bowl, with clay and bone ash. Then into it went crude ores and slag which contained some silver and gold as well as base metals like lead. Then they made a fire and fanned it, with bellows, to a quick, intense heat. The lead and other base metals were oxidized by the heat and sank into the porous bottom and sides of the cupel, leaving crude silver and gold, still combined, in the bottom.

The second process, known as "cementation," took place in furnaces nearby. There the ancient refinery workers heated the two metals together, in contact, to effect a change in one of them, and separated the two. Cementation is still sometimes used today to form steel by heating iron in powdered charcoal.

There was no doubt that this had been a refinery, but it became important to establish its date. Ramage and a colleague attacked the heap of slag and debris again, hunting for pottery or ceramics that might be datable. Plowing through piles of broken and burned brick, chunks of lead oxide, and plain old rocks and dirt, they found the ceramic fragments they sought and lifted them carefully out of the dump heap. Scientific and stylistic testing both revealed that the pottery had been made in the years 570 B.C. to 550 B.C.

And King Croesus, the stories all say, ruled from 560 B.C. to 546 B.C. Another legend had come alive, on the banks of the storied little Pactolus River.

15

A VERY EARLY "BIBLE BELT"

Just south of the modern city of Izmir, near the ruins of once-great Ephesus, a new road wriggles off toward the hills. It winds around the foot of Bulbul Dagh (Mt. Nightingale), where one can still see the massive walls and towers that were built in the fourth century B.C. to help defend Ephesus. But the road doesn't go there. It is marked to "Meryem Ana," the Turkish words for "the house of Mary." Here, many believe, the Virgin Mary spent the last years of her life and here she died, to be taken directly to heaven.

A little stone chapel stands on the site, simple and appealing in the shade of an enormous plane tree. Visitors arrive in a parking lot several yards away, where signs admonish them, in several languages, that in this place there shall be no unseemly noise, no picnics, no reclining on the grass, and no radio playing. Both admission and parking are free, however. In the Moslem world, Jesus Christ is not the son of God, but He is a prophet, and His mother is to be respected. The walk toward the little stone "house" goes between olive trees, and every few steps there is another large neat sign giving the history of the site itself. There are signs in Turkish, German, English, Spanish, French, Greek, and Italian.

The so-called House of Mary outside Ephesus, where the Virgin Mary is supposed to have spent her last days. The stone structure is a little chapel and covers some first-century ruins of the house itself.

Inside are stone walls and stone floors, a small altar with candles burning, and the abandoned crutches of pilgrims who believe they were miraculously cured in the House of Mary. Most of the structure actually dates from the sixth century of the Christian Era, but archaeologists believe bits of the foundation are much earlier, from some time in the first century after Christ.

There are two other sites in the Mediterranean that claim the Virgin Mary as well. One is the Church of the Dormition on Mt. Zion in Jerusalem, on the spot where Mary, so some say, died at the age of sixty-three. The other is Loreto, in Italy, where, according to legend, the House of the Virgin landed miraculously in 1295, having been blown all the way from Nazareth. The claims of the Church of the Dormition are based on an eighth-century manuscript that has seldom seemed very reliable to scholars, and the claims of Loreto are of course even more dubious, though they provided the basis fifty years ago of a papal proclamation making the Madonna of Loreto the protector of aviators. This seems appropriate, even if not very logical.

There is no solution in the Bible to the geographical question of just where Mary died. The Scriptures are completely silent about the latter part of her life. All we are told is that Christ on the Cross entrusted his mother to his beloved John, "and from that moment the disciple took her into his home." It is historically true that after Christ's death his followers were persecuted in Jerusalem. St. Stephen was stoned; St. James was beheaded. The remaining disciples divided the known world into territories and assigned one disciple to each region for preaching the Gospel. John was assigned to Asia Minor, and if he considered Jerusalem too dangerous for Mary, he would likely have taken her with him. John's association with Ephesus is clear and unmistakable. He is known to have been in Ephesus in A.D. 67, and he is believed to have been buried there, on a hillside a bit removed from the major ruins of the old city. In the sixth century after Christ, the Emperor Justinian constructed an enormous Church of St. John on the traditional site of his tomb.

In A.D. 48 John is known to have been in Jerusalem, but in the years 37 to 48 his whereabouts are undocumented. It is possible that he went to Ephesus in those earlier years, taking Mary with him, and that he returned to Jerusalem in 48 and went back to Ephesus in 67. St. Paul, who made three trips to Ephesus and actually lived in the city for more than two years between A.D. 55 and 58, is said to have found churches already established there when he arrived. Who could have founded these early groups? The hypothesis is that it was John, with Mary still under his care.

Further strong hints that Mary was in Ephesus come from the fact that in A.D. 431 the Third Ecumenical Council of the Christian Church was held in Ephesus in a basilica called the Church of the Virgin Mary. In the early days of the Church, places of worship were almost always dedicated to persons who had lived or died very near the site. Furthermore, it was the council of 431 that proclaimed the dogma of "Mary, Mother of God," as well as

proclaiming the divinity of Christ himself. The 431 council was
a very stormy one, and as a result its records have come down to
us in some detail through the centuries. No sooner had the prel-
ates of Christianity met together than they got into an argument.
The majority wished to establish that Jesus was both God *and*
man, and wished to declare the dogma of Mary. In opposition
was Nestorius, the Patriarch of Constantinople. He and his fac-
tion lost the argument; Nestorius was charged with heresy and
cast out of the church. To this day that famous dispute in
Ephesus has remained a symbol of schism and the name of a sect,
the Nestorians.

As the centuries passed, Christianity was largely superseded
in Turkey by the Moslem religion, but a haunting folk memory
and a tradition lingered. The old Christians of Ephesus told
their children, and their grandchildren, from one generation to
the next, that Mary had both lived and died here. The descendants of those early Christians made a pilgrimage every year on
August 15, the date celebrated in Roman Catholic countries as
the Assumption of the Virgin, to the hills of Ephesus. Pope Bene-
dict XIV (1740–1758) helped to make their faith official by de-
creeing that Mary had died in Ephesus, and in 1967 the present
Pope, Paul VI, made his own pilgrimage to the ancient city to the
Church of St. John and the House of Mary.

For centuries, however, no trace of the Virgin's tomb or of any
home that might have been hers ever turned up in Ephesus, and
the yearly August 15 pilgrims had no specific place to go. This
situation changed, startlingly, in the nineteenth century. An inva-
lid German nun wrote a book called *Life of the Blessed Virgin
Mary*, in which she describes in great detail the last home and its
surroundings. The information had come to her in a vision, she
said. The nun (1774–1824) was named Catherine Emmerich. She
had never been to Ephesus; she had never been out of her own
country, and she had been bedridden for twelve years. Eventually
the book was translated, and it came to the attention of several
priests and monks who had been to Ephesus and knew the site
well. By the nineteenth century, archaeologists had begun excavating the remarkable Greek and Roman ruins, and Biblical
scholars had studied them. The learned priests were struck im-

mediately by the resemblance between Catherine Emmerich's unidentified "last home" and the physical site of Ephesus itself. By 1891, interest in the description in the book, plus the growing suspicion of students that there must be some connection between the physical presence of the Virgin and the coincidence of the basilica named for her and the Ecumenical Council in Ephesus, set off a search for any visible remains of a home that could have been hers. On a beautiful hilly site, nestled in trees and overlooking the glittering sea, they found the remains of a sixth-century structure built on first-century foundations. It fitted the nun's description almost perfectly.

This, then, is the present House of Mary. Whatever its qualifications for the title, it is a most beguiling place, a charming locale to imagine as the last earthly home of the Mother of Jesus even though, as writer Freya Stark has wryly pointed out (in *Ionia, a Quest*, John Murray Publishers, 1954), "the Mother of God must have been extremely robust to get up here through roadless scrub at the age—presumably—of ninety or near it."

There has been a persistent belief, in Ephesus, that this city is the home of the Mother of Gods. It began long before Christianity . . . it began with the goddess Cybele, beloved of so many long-vanished nations of Anatolia. Cybele's mantle passed, with the coming of the Greeks, to their own goddess Artemis, and here in Ephesus they erected a temple to Artemis which was so magnificent it was one of the Seven Wonders of the World. The Romans renamed Artemis for their own goddess Diana, and when they became Christian they helped dismantle the great Temple of Artemis to build the Byzantine church of St. John. Yet the dream, the wish, the belief that this site is holy has gone on for more than three thousand years.

If ever there was a historical "Bible belt" to rival Israel itself, to span the years and beliefs of both Testaments, and to send the diggers out to prove that the Gospel is gospel, it is the western and southern shore of today's Turkey. Giants from the Old Testement walked these dusty roads, or ones very like them; nomads camped as some tribes do today. Turkish tradition insists that the patriarch Abraham actually died and was buried in a cave near

Ephesus, another storied city of the ancients, is being restored by a German-Austrian expedition. The Temple of Hadrian, one of the handsomest structures in the city, was built by Romans in A.D. *117–138.*

A marble, seen in the Ephesus Archaeological Museum, of the goddess Artemis, whose temple was one of the Seven Wonders of the Ancient World.

the modern town of Urfa, just over the border from Iraq, and
that his bones were later removed to Israel. Abraham is a prophet
in the Moslem religion, and Turkish legend says he almost perished ahead of his time in an encounter with an arrogant local
king called Nimrod—or Nemrud: versions vary. This king had
such a bad reputation that modern Turks still use his name to
frighten their children into circumspect behavior. Nimrod once
captured the prophet Abraham, they say, and tied him to a stake
to burn him. At the crucial moment a storm came up, put out the
fire, saved Abraham, and created a small lake at the site. There
is still a small lake near Urfa, fed by springs, which drains into
the Euphrates River. Fish grow in the lake and leap out of the
water to eat lettuce from the hands of believers who come to the
water to be cured of physical ailments. The fish are, pious Turkish peasants assure the visitor, the reincarnation of the sticks of
wood with which the wicked Nimrod meant to burn Abraham.

This story is as delightful, and about as credible, as the flight
of the Virgin's house to Loreto. A more scholarly search for the
burial place of Abraham goes back to the account in Genesis
which describes how Abraham buried his wife Sarah in "the
cave of Machpelah," which has been traced to the ancient town
of Hebron, south of Jerusalem, now in the territory of Israel.
Here, Biblical archaeologists believe, were buried not only Sarah
but also Abraham himself, Isaac, Rebekah, Leah, and Jacob. In
the twelfth century at least one pilgrim wrote of having been
taken to the site, then a Crusader church devoted to "St. Abraham," and having paid money to see the tombs of the patriarchs.

The connection of Turkey with the figures and events of the
New Testament is far more specific and detailed. Once Jesus had
lived and died, his disciples swarmed out of their corner of the
ancient world, impelled by a fever to spread the good word and
hastened on their way by merciless persecution at home. They did
not rush en masse to Rome, however, or even to Greece, though
most of the early versions of the New Testament were written
in Greek. Many of them set forth for lands much nearer home:
for the Biblical Antioch, which is today's Turkish Antakya; for
Ephesus; for Tarsus. It was in what is today Turkey that the word
"Christian" was first used. In The Acts of the Apostles, written
by St. Luke, is an account of how Barnabas went from Jerusalem

to Antioch and there found people who believed in "the Way," as the new religion was often then called. In Acts 11, Luke says, "and in Antioch the disciples were for the first time called Christians."

It was in Tarsus, in southern Turkey, that Saul was born. Saul, who began his life by persecuting Christians, was converted on the road to Damascus, and lived to become the Paul of the Gospels, the most prolific letter writer of the New Testament. Luke tells the whole story in Acts: how Saul hounded men and women to death or to prison for their faith; how he was blinded by a great light on the way to Damascus and heard a voice from heaven saying, "Saul, Saul, why do you persecute me?" And the terrified Saul asked, "Who are you?"—to which the voice replied, "I am Jesus of Nazareth."

Saul saw the light in more ways than one. He became a convert, changed his name to Paul, and was the most indefatigable disciple of them all. He roamed the civilized world tirelessly preaching his message. He preached in Greece and in Rome, and he almost perished in a shipwreck so graphically described in the Bible (Acts 27:15, 27–29) that underwater archaeologists still study the passage today to gain insight as to where to look, among the reefs of the ancient sea lanes, for other wrecks of the period.

Paul preached often in Ephesus, and there one day his faith ran head on into one of the earlier religions of the great city. It was a historic encounter. Most people in Ephesus, around A.D. 50, still worshiped the Mother Goddess figure of the Greek Artemis. Artemis' great shrine had become an attraction for thousands of pilgrims, and it had become a source of very brisk business in souvenirs and little replicas of the goddess of the holy place. This is a situation not entirely unknown even in our own era. Into all this came Paul, preaching and teaching to all who would listen the new religion of Jesus of Nazareth, a religion that he was sure would replace all others in the hearts of men.

This greatly upset the priests of Artemis, and it upset the makers of souvenirs. It was a silversmith named Demetrius who actually set off the commotion. The Biblical account of Demetrius and what he wrought, as set down in Acts, is as dramatic as a breathless twentieth-century TV report of a near-riot:

"About that time there arose no little stir concerning the Way," the story begins. "For a man named Demetrius, a silversmith, who made silver shrines of Artemis, brought no little business to the craftsmen. These he gathered together, with the workmen of like occupation, and said, 'Men, you know that from this business we have our wealth. And you see and hear that not only at Ephesus but almost throughout all Asia this Paul has persuaded and turned away a considerable company of people, saying that gods made with hands are not gods. And there is danger not only that this trade of ours may come into disrepute but also that the temple of the great goddess Artemis may count for nothing, and that she may even be deposed from her magnificence, she whom all Asia and the world worship.'

"When they heard all this they were enraged, and cried out, 'Great is Artemis of the Ephesians!' So the city was filled with great confusion; and they rushed into the theater, dragging with them . . . Paul's companions."

The "theater" into which Demetrius and his companions rushed has now been identified by archaeologists and Biblical historians as an ancient Greek structure which the Romans had decided to renovate to make it conform to their own ideas of stagecraft. The alteration began in A.D. 40 and went on for decades. So on the day of Demetrius' near-riot it must have been full of workmen banging away with their chisels or straining at ropes to maneuver blocks of stone into place. Their astonishment when the populace of Ephesus erupted into the theater shouting and yelling must have been something to behold. One can easily imagine them first looking up, then looking at each other, then happily putting down their tools and relaxing in the shade to hear what the uproar was all about.

As usual, when a mob of people gets excited, there was a certain amount of disorganization. The account in Acts says that "Now some cried one thing, some another; for the assembly was in confusion, and most of them did not know why they had come together. . . ."

Paul himself wanted to rush to the theater to argue with Demetrius, but his friends begged him not to go, and he took their advice. In the end, the near-riot was calmed by the good sense of a nameless "town clerk" who stood up to insist that "We are in danger of being charged with rioting today, there being no cause that we can give to justify this commotion." Anyone who had any legitimate charges against the man Paul, he said should do so by legal, orderly means: "The courts are open, and there are pro-consuls." (The translation of The Acts of the Apostles quoted above is taken from *The Bible Reader*, Bruce Books, New York, 1969.)

The crowd at Ephesus thereupon dispersed with no bloodshed, but the anger of the silversmiths and the craftsmen did not diminish. So Paul, having first given elaborate instructions to his disciples, prudently moved on to Macedonia.

A great many of the epistles of Paul, and of the other books of the Bible so laboriously memorized by generations of Sunday-school children, were written either from Turkey or to Turkey by the pioneers of the church. Paul wrote First Corinthians from Ephesus, and from prison in Rome he wrote Ephesians back to Ephesus. Galatians was written to churches in central Turkey, and Colossians to a group of faithful near the present town of Denizli. The book of Timothy was a letter to a friend he had left in charge of the church in Ephesus, and First Peter was Peter's letter to persecuted Christians in the north of present Turkey.

Revelations, as we often refer to it, is more accurately described as The Revelation to John, and it was addressed specifically to the "seven churches of Asia," all of them located within 100 miles of what is now Izmir, Turkey. This very complicated and confusing book, full of outlandish images and complex symbolism in numbers, strange beasts, stars, and the like, is supposed to have come to John in a series of visions, or "revelations," which the Lord sent to his disciple. John writes that a voice like a trumpet from heaven commanded him to "Write what you see in a book, and send it to the seven churches, to Ephesus and to Smyrna and to Pergamum and to Thyatira and to Sardis and to Philadelphia and to Laodicea." The famous seven stars and seven golden lamp stands of one part of the vision refer to those seven churches and to the "angels" thereof. There is within The Revelation a specific letter, or message, to each church.

The vivid, enigmatic images of The Revelation have inspired a stream of poems, hymns, folk music, paintings, and preachers

● Canakkale

● Bursa

The "Seven Churches of Asia"

The modern names are in roman type, the Biblical names in italics.

● Bergama
Pergamum

● Akhisar
Thyatira

● Izmir
Smyrna

● Sart
Sardis

● Alasehir
Philadelphia

● Selçuk
Ephesus

Aegean Sea

● Denizli
Laodicea

Kilometers   0   40   80

TARSUS ⟶
185 miles

(some of the latter as wild-eyed as the visions themselves) for all of the two millennia since the book was written. From them come the mosaic of Jesus in Majesty that decorates the Shrine of the Immaculate Conception in Washington, D.C., and the magnificent fourteenth-century tapestries of Angers, France. From The Revelation come the "Four Horsemen of the Apocalypse," whose image has graced everything from painting to sculpture to the Notre Dame backfield.

How very large the "seven churches of Asia" must therefore have loomed, in the early days of Christianity. Almost all the names have changed, and most of the physical remains of those early churches have vanished, yet still today in Turkey a devout tourist may easily arrange a visit to all seven. Ephesus, Sardis, Smyrna (modern Izmir), and Pergamum we have discussed briefly in this book. Thyatira is now called Akhisar on the maps, and Philadelphia has become modern Alasehir. Perhaps the most interesting of the lesser-known ones is ancient Laodicea, which was located near the present city of Denizli. This was a crossroads of the world in St. Paul's day, very near to Colossae, to whose citizens he wrote Colossians, and to a Roman city called Hierapolis. The ruins of Hierapolis remain today, massively Roman and magnificently preserved, near Denizli. They stand, furthermore, in a landscape as fantastic as The Revelation itself: a 300-foot-high series of cliffs which look like a frozen waterfall. They glitter white in the sun, red in the sunset, and down the side of each is a series of pools which look like dead-white saucers slipped into the cliffsides by the hand of a magic giant. The Turks call the place Pamukkale, "the cotton fortress," and at the time of Christ the local citizens believed that the waters of this strange cliffside had magic properties. The Romans built enormous baths there, utilizing the natural hot water with its high mineral content. Today's tourists can swim in one of the deepest of the natural pools, and in a man-made one nearby can glide and drift in absolutely clear water among the tumbled columns and capitals of ancient Roman buildings.

The miracle of the "cotton fortress" is a natural one. The whole upthrust series of cliffs is laced with veins through which lime-rich water flows in streams and trickles. As it heads down-

Turks call this site Pamukkale, "the cotton fortress," because of the strange patterns made by mineral-laden waters coming down the mountainside, forming stalactites as the water trickles from one level to another.

ward toward the valley 300 feet below, it leaves a lime deposit wherever it passes. The deposits build up into saucerlike formations, then spill over to make stalactites, which in turn are stained red or green by other mineral deposits and begin to form a new saucer just below.

The Revelation's message to the church at Laodicea, near Pamukkale, is as obscure as is most of that particular book of the Bible, yet in a strange way it seems to indicate that the Lord knew all about the region when he sent the vision to John. "I know your works," John wrote to Laodicea; "you are neither cold nor hot. Would that you were cold or hot!" Nowadays the water, at least, is both cold *and* hot.

Perhaps the most intriguing of all Biblical references and mysteries in Turkey is that of Noah's Ark. The book of Genesis states

Stalactite formations.

clearly that after the deluge of 40 days and 40 nights, and after the waters had prevailed over all the earth for more than 150 days, they began at last to go down and "the ark came to rest upon the mountains of Ararat." The geographical reference is unmistakable. Throughout recorded history an area of eastern Turkey, near where the present boundaries of Turkey, Iraq, and the Soviet Union meet, has been known as the region of Ararat. Well within this area, just north of Lake Van, is a towering volcanic peak called Mt. Ararat, 17,000 feet high.

Periodically, almost as often as someone reports a UFO in the skies, there is an excited announcement that somebody has found a piece of the ark on the mountainside, or has sighted its remains from an airplane.

So, naturally, the first time I got even remotely near to Mt. Ararat, I asked Turkish friends about the ark. They shook their heads. It is a very unfriendly mountain, they said. It is barren almost all the way from foot to summit; it generates fierce storms and blinding fogs with little warning; its volcanic rumblings and belching produce clouds of sulfurous steam which melt the glaciers and send huge rocks hurtling down on the heads of climbers. Sometimes in summer even tourists can master the gentle south slope, but there are wolves and bears. Then, as if all that weren't enough to discourage the curious, they announced that, besides, it was a military zone, owing to its proximity to the Soviet border, and people couldn't go there without special permission.

But—in Turkey, as in most of the Mediterranean, there is always a "but"—they had a friend who was an expert on the ark. In due course they produced him: Turkish army Major Sahap Atalay. Major Atalay is more than six feet tall, handsome, suntanned, muscular, mustachioed. When he smiles his teeth flash like sun on water, and he smiles a lot. Yes, he had known Mt. Ararat well for more than twenty years. He had climbed it Allah knows how many times. His military duties often took him there, and he had often served as guide and expedition director for ark-hunters approved by the Turkish government. Had he ever seen anything that looked like the remains of the ark? Major Atalay smiled again. "I suggest," he said softly, "that you discuss this matter with your countryman John Libi. He lives in San Francisco."

John Libi, now seventy-seven, has been obsessed by the dream of Noah's Ark since he was a little boy. He thinks it was "because my mother was a religious woman," but it is more likely that he caught the dream, without ever knowing it, from the tales of the peasants and the folklore of the land where he grew up. He was born Ivan Kirov, son of Russian parents, in Bulgaria. That isn't so far from Mt. Ararat, and young Ivan was Turkish-speaking, as are many Bulgarians, so he was steeped in the tall tales of his corner of the world. He emigrated to the United States as a young man, changed his name to John Libi, and began a wandering life which led him eventually to San Francisco and a job as an elevator operator. Some say he practiced for his assault on Mt. Ararat by running up and down the stairs of the building when there was no call for the elevator, but Libi denies this tale.

He first scaled the mountain to look for the ark in 1954. He was already near sixty, and worried Turkish officials assigned him a young lieutenant named Sahap Atalay, who Libi confesses "almost carried me, some of the times." They actually tried twice that year, and Libi has headed for Mt. Ararat seven times since. He must be the unluckiest would-be archaeologist in all the world. One climb was called off after he got to Turkey on the ground that it was "militarily inadvisable." That was in internationally tense 1955. In 1958, the hapless Libi fell 40 feet from a rocky ledge and had to be carried down to a hospital. Once he got pneumonia while near the peak; once he lost a week looking for the body of a young Belgian climber who had insisted upon rushing ahead of the main party and been killed. Once he ended up in a snow bank treacherous as quicksand and was rescued by Atalay (by now a captain), who worked himself as near as possible in the mushy snow, hooked an arm around an outcrop of rock, and extended the stock of his rifle to Libi to catch hold of and pull himself out by. Bad weather, everything from thunderstorms to snowstorms, drove him off the mountain several times, and in 1962 Libi didn't even get as far as Turkey, because he stopped in Italy en route and pickpockets slit both rear pockets of his trousers and made off with the funds for the expedition.

Worst of all, however, was the climb of the bears. Libi tells it dramatically in his picturesque English: "We were about eleven thousand feet of the altitude and we come to the glacier that is up there. Sahap and the others say they want to go have a look on the Russian side and they take the guns and I have something, a shovel I guess, for weapon. There was snow all around but also sand and in the sun it was hot and I felt kind of sick. Every few minutes I have to get up and drink water. They left at one o'clock and they told me they'd be back by four o'clock. At about three o'clock I see them coming back from the snow, there some kind of slope, and I see these two fellows my friends coming back. So I open my big mouth and call out in Turkish, 'I'm here!' Then these fellows come closer, about eight hundred feet, and they were two brown bears. I thought they was big as horses, and I made them twice as big. Soon as I see them I got cured. I try to camouflage, I roll down and jump rocks, I kill my arms and legs but good thing. When I got far enough away I look back and the bears were sitting where I was before, just sitting. So I climbed on and I didn't look back for the bears and I came to a shepherd's house. They kept me there and at night Sahap he sent two soldiers and they fired their rifles for a signal and we got together again.

"They had stopped where they had left me and they saw the bear steps but didn't see any blood and they wonder what the bears did with me. My friend Sahap he was so worried he couldn't even eat.

"All the newspapers later made some fun with my bears. Somebody wrote that the bears threw rocks at us but that wasn't true. That was another time, when I was just alone with Sahap and big rocks, things that looked like Roman columns came down the mountain and we were both scared but they stopped, just before hit us. I wasn't scared so much that day, but I was plenty scared of the bears. Afterward some papers said that John Libi didn't find the ark but he sure found the bears who were in it."

Accident-prone but courageous John Libi has never found the ark, in nine tries, and he has never even found pieces of wood from it. His only regret is that he has spent all his spare money on his fruitless expeditions, and now he fears he is too old to try

John Libi, the intrepid ark-hunter, on Mt. Ararat in 1965, standing about 3,000 feet from the summit.

again. Yet he remains convinced, as are almost all who seek the ark, that he knows exactly where it is. The precise location came to him in a dream in 1958 when he was on the S.S. *Olympia* going from New York to Greece:

"I dreamed that it was about nine A.M. and I was standing on the deck. I noticed a freighter about a hundred yards from our ship, traveling in the same direction and at the same speed, on a glassy sea. Suddenly this freighter churned up some mud and seemed to be stuck and then I noticed that it rose up out of the sea and the mountain rose with it for hundreds of feet. There was the freighter on top of this mountain. There was a large man near me and I called to his attention that the freighter was stuck on top and he said in a very loud voice that the freighter was going to stay there. At the same time I noticed that the water was going down hundreds of feet; of course it was actually the mountain coming up, several hundred feet. I was so frightened that I woke up, but it is that dream which showed me where the ark is. My relationship to that freighter is exactly the same position as the ark is on the mountain. I was in that same spot in the first climb in 1954. That was when the big rock fell from the top and buried itself on the side only about thirty to forty feet from us. We were able to pass by safely to the top and we searched the top but we were unsuccessful. I know now that the ark is where that rock fell and stopped. It was a kind of sign, see, and then it came back in my dream. . . ."

Signs there have always been, and reports, some quite sober and some highly fanciful. An obscure historian of 475 B.C. named Berosus said that inhabitants of the Ararat region had scraped the pitch covering from the planks and ribs of the ark and used it in little lumps as good-luck charms and antidotes for ailments. The Jewish historian Josephus, who lived at the time of Christ, wrote that the ark's "remains are shown there by the inhabitants to this day." Even Marco Polo, the fourteenth-century world traveler, claimed to have been to look at the area. He doesn't come right out and say that he saw the ark, but he mentions its existence, near the summit of Mt. Ararat.

A Russian physician climbed the mountain in 1829 and said he had found wood there. So did an archbishop in 1892—he said the wood was "dark red." This is important, because there is no native wood at all near the top of the mountain. Commercial aviators flying over the area in the twentieth century reported seeing "boatlike shapes" on Mt. Ararat and on nearby peaks as well.

It remained for a Frenchman named Fernand Navarra to bring back "a piece of the ark" for the first time. Navarra has recounted that he first heard about Noah's Ark from his parents, when they tried to distract him from the fright of a near-drowning when he was five years old. Just how much comfort the whole story of near-universal drowning could have been to a soggy small boy seems doubtful, but it certainly lodged Noah in young Fernand's mind. From that moment on, he says, he was determined to find the ark. Chance, or one of John Libi's "signs," entered his life when he was twenty and doing his military service. In the army, he met an Armenian named Alim. Mt. Ararat stands in territory that was once Armenia, and Alim showed his excited young friend maps of the area. He described the mountain, and he assured Fernand that the ark was there. But, said Alim, only someone who was "innocent as a child" would ever succeed in finding it.

Fernand Navarra didn't forget that remark. He finished his military service, made a modest fortune as a demolition engineer, had six children, and dreamed of the ark. When he had accumulated enough money to finance an expedition, he went. Twice he climbed Mt. Ararat and twice he found nothing. Then in 1955, accompanied by an eleven-year-old son who could qualify for Alim's "innocent as a child," he went back. And this time he announced to a startled world that he had found the ark. On the morning of July 6, 1955, he reported, he emerged early from his camp tent at almost 14,000 feet up the mountain and lowered himself into a crevasse with the sort of rope ladder used by spelunkers, the people who explore underground caverns. There, all around him, was a dark mass of material which looked like wood, and it was shaped like a ship. It was locked into an ancient, immobile mass of packed snow and ice. Navarra attacked the mass with an ice axe and managed to hack through enough of it to expose one timber. He sawed off about 5 feet of the timber, thanked his son Raphael for having provided the "innocence" that led him to the ark, tied the timber sideways across his shoulders, and trekked back down the mountain.

Back in France, Navarra excitedly wrote about his find and, like a good archaeologist, submitted it to tests. A forestry institute in Madrid, Spain, studied a sample of the wood and estimated its age at 5,000 years. A technical laboratory for wood in Paris estimated 4,484 years, and an institute of prehistory in Bordeaux was content simply to report that the wood was of "great antiquity."

These estimates were old enough, in all probability, to reach back to the era of the Great Deluge. There were, however, some technical problems. The wood, in testing, turned out to be white oak, while the Bible says that Noah used a resinous wood and some experts have guessed that it must have been cypress. An even more telling point was that oak does not grow for hundreds of miles in the vicinity of Mt. Ararat.

Fernand Navarra brushed aside the quibbles. Who knew, after all, precisely where Noah had built his ark and how far it had drifted before it came to rest on the mountaintop? He estimated that there were fifty tons of ancient wood locked in the ice and choked with the fallen boulders of millennia, and he wanted to go back to Ararat with proper equipment to try to figure out a way to measure the ship and to extract it. He even wrote a book about his "discovery of the ark," and this came to the attention of a U.S. group called the SEARCH Foundation, Inc. (Scientific Exploration and Research), of Washington, D.C.

SEARCH offered to mount an expedition and help Navarra go back to the mountain. After years of fund-raising and of delicate negotiations with the Turkish government, an exploration party set forth in 1969. Accompanied by Turkish guides and led by Navarra, its members climbed up to 14,000 feet and then looked for the crevasse into which Navarra said he had lowered himself on that July day fourteen years earlier. They could not find it. Navarra remembered the way, but the crevasse was closed, either by a slight movement of the ice mass or by snow accumulation in all those years. He and the members of the party did find a place beside the glacier in which a trickle of melting ice had formed a pool. They probed the pool and found several pieces of planking, very much weathered and quite fragmentary. The largest piece was about 18 inches long, 4 inches wide and an inch thick. Yet it had been unmistakably worked by hand, and it looked very old indeed.

They had not found the main body of the enormous timbers Navarra had described, but they had found wood. The party returned to the United States and then submitted samples of both 1955 and 1969 wood for further testing, this time by American experts. The University of California, the Geochron Laboratories in Cambridge, Massachusetts, and the University of Pennsylvania all tested the age of the wood by the Carbon-14 method. And all reported that it was from 1,300 to 1,700 years old. *Not half old enough to have come from Noah's ark.*

Bravely facing these reports, the SEARCH Foundation issued a news release about them. They headed the release, however, with the words "Distinct Possibility Ararat Wood May Be Part of Noah's Ark." Their argument was that the U.S. Carbon-14 method in this particular instance might have been made inaccurate by the peculiar circumstances that exist on top of Mt. Ararat. The wood, they said, had been soaked in glacial melt water for many centuries, being impregnated with the sulfuric acid and gases emitted by the still-active volcano itself. This could alter the amounts of Carbon-14 in the wood and throw off the measurements. The methods used by the European wood testers who had dated Navarra's plank at about five thousand years old, they said, were based on such things as the degree of lignite formation, the modification of cells within the wood, the degree of fossilization, and other factors.

This announcement by SEARCH was viewed with suspicion in some scientific quarters, and for a reason that seldom arises these days in scientific discussions: religion. SEARCH, though it is based in Washington, D.C., is a private organization which gets its funds from appeals to the public. Many of its members are Seventh-Day Adventists, whose church tends to adopt a far more literal interpretation of the Bible than do most other religious sects. Many of the people who contribute to the valuable explorations conducted by SEARCH do so in the hope that these explorations will prove every word of the Bible to be literally, specifically correct. Thus these supporters would *want* the planks and the wood fragments to be 5,000 years old, rather than a mere 1,700 years, or 1,300 years.

Once the question of the age of Fernand Navarra's plank and SEARCH's wood fragment had been raised, criticisms of "the Noah's Ark theory" came from many sources. John Libi in San Francisco hinted that Navarra had carried that 1955 plank up the mountain with him and then carried it back down again. A party of six Italian mountaineers came back from Mt. Ararat in 1970 and said that two Turkish guides had told them, unequivocally, that Navarra's find was a hoax. He had provided his own wood and then had had his picture taken carrying it down the mountain, they said. A group of Turkish climbers struggled up to the biggest of the famous "boat shapes" seen from airplanes over Mt. Ararat and reported that what looked concave from the air was convex when seen on the ground: the "hollow" of a boat was in fact a grassy hillock surrounded by rocks. This is a phenomenon now familiar to those who have studied photographs of the moon. The "craters" often actually look like little mountains instead of hollows.

Historians and archaeologists recall that centuries ago there had been a monastery at the foot of Mt. Ararat, dedicated to a monk now called St. Jacob. This man sought the ark, and three times he tried to climb the mountain. Each time he got part way up and then was overwhelmed by a sleep so irresistible that he closed his eyes. And each time when he woke up he was back at the bottom again. Finally, the legend says, he was visited by an angel who told him that the mountain was holy and that he could never climb it. But to reward him for his persistence the angel intended to give him one plank from the ark, and the angel laid the plank on the tired monk's chest. The monk became a saint, and the plank became the centerpiece of a monastery built on the spot. The monastery was destroyed by fire in about A.D. 653. If there were fragments of the wood left from that fire, and if they had somehow got from the monastery up the side of Mt. Ararat, they would fit the date given by the U.S. universities to the wood brought down by Navarra and the SEARCH Foundation.

And yet . . . and yet. There is no doubt in the mind of either historian or archaeologist, of whatever religious persuasion, that once there was a flood. A deluge. Maybe a Noah figure and an Ark.

This was proved, one hundred years ago, in a story as dramatic as that of Schliemann at Troy or Mellaart on the Turkish train, by a very young Englishman prosaically named George Smith. Smith was born to poor parents and was apprenticed when very young to an engraver, to learn to make proper engravings from which bank notes were printed. He seems to have been very good at his job, but his true passion was the Bible, especially the Old Testament. He read it and reread it, he studied every book of Near Eastern writing he could find, and he was fond of repeating, over and over, "the Bible is right." His scholarship brought him to the attention of the Keeper of the British Museum, who appointed young Smith at only twenty-one to act as a restorer at the museum. The first job he was given there was to put back together an enormous heap of broken clay tablets that a British expedition was digging up at the site of Nineveh in what is now Iraq, near the Turkish border. Smith began innocently enough piecing together the bits of clay which were incised with the strange "nails and wedges" of cuneiform writing. The lines reminded him of copper engravings, and as he worked he began to learn the little symbols.

It was the era in which cuneiform was beginning to be read by the great code-breakers of nineteenth-century England, and Smith spent all his spare time studying the texts and translations. Before long he was able to read the clay tablets he was gluing back together again. He could read them almost as well as the experts, and he stayed late at night to do this. His chief complaint was the London fog, which so dimmed the light of his oil lamp that he had to give up early and go home.

Most of the tablets he worked with were dreary inventories of commercial transactions or accounts of the grand deeds of long-dead monarchs, but one night in the British Museum, Smith realized that he was reading an epic. It was the account of a man named Gilgamesh, clearly the hero of the story, who was two parts divine and one part human. This Gilgamesh was trying to rebuild some walls and temples of his native city of Uruk, and the inhabitants, who resented having to work so hard for him, complained to the gods.

On and on the epic went, telling of Gilgamesh's enemy Enkidu, of how the two eventually became friends. Then Enkidu died, of some strange malady, and Gilgamesh was heartbroken. He was also scared, but he knew whom to ask for advice on how to escape death. He would ask an ancestor, a man named Ut-napishtim, who had been the sole survivor of the Deluge.

The Deluge? Bible-reading George Smith nearly leaped out of his chair. There had been only one Deluge, and Noah had been its hero. It was all in the Bible. And yet these clay tablets, from Nineveh, were much older than the Bible. Feverishly Smith sorted through his heaps of tablets, but the story ended here. The piece he was reading was broken off, just as he was about to decipher this story of the Great Flood.

He had seen enough to fire his imagination, however. On December 3, 1872, he addressed the august members of the Society of Biblical Archaeology in London. He told them that he had news of a Babylonian Deluge, and the announcement spread through archaeology-loving England like a brush fire. There were articles in the press, there was excitement in the clubs. The London *Daily Telegraph* offered a grand prize of 1,000 pounds (a lot of money in 1872) to anyone who could find the missing pieces of what had already become known as the "Gilgamesh Epic." Probably, the scholars thought, the pieces would be somewhere in the excavations at Nineveh where diggers were still sifting through the library of the palace of a king called Ashurnasirpal. There on the site was a mountain of clay fragments. Could anyone find the missing pieces? Could they have been thrown away early in the digging because they were so fragmented or so illegible?

George Smith seemed to be the only man who could read the tablets at sight, and the only one who knew for sure what he was looking for. So the British Museum sent him out to try to win the 1,000 pounds. No bookmaker in the London of 1872—or the London of 1972—would have given 1,000 to 1 that young Smith would find his fragment. Yet, by what still seems a miracle, he did. On a spring day in 1873, he held it in his hands—a bit of clay with less than twenty lines of cuneiform writing on it. They were lines of explosive import: the opening passage of the Deluge. They recounted how the gods decided to destroy the whole human race to punish it for its sins. One of the gods, who still felt friendly toward mankind, contrived to send a dream to one of his favorite humans called Ut-napishtim. He warned Ut-napishtim what was going to happen, and advised him to build a boat for himself, his family, a boat pilot, and the "seeds of life of all the species." Ut-napishtim did as he was told, and then the skies opened and "everything human was transformed into mud." Ut-napishtim's boat drifted for only six days and seven nights, and then landed on the top of "Mt. Nisir." Ut-napishtim, like Noah, sent out messengers, a dove and a swallow, and both came back because they could find no dry land upon which to perch. Then he sent a raven, which did not return, and Ut-napishtim and his family and the ship's pilot got out and lived happily ever after.

The Gilgamesh Epic has now been dated to about four thousand years ago. It is eerily like the Biblical account of the flood, although Noah in the Bible did not require a pilot, and although the Gilgamesh text refers to "gods" instead of the later, Judeo-Christian idea of a single God. The length of time involved varies in the two versions, and Ut-napishtim is supposed to have made a "rich sacrifice" to his protector when things dried out a bit. Yet the implication is clear: this story of the Flood predates the Biblical account, and in so doing helps tremendously to "prove" it.

Few believe today that any deluge could bury "all the earth" and drown every living thing except the inhabitants of a ship. But how big is any man's world, and how big was it at the time of the Deluge? Both versions of the flood story place the scene of action near the junction of the mightiest rivers of the ancient world, the Tigris and the Euphrates, and calamitous floods must often have all but obliterated the only horizons the ancients knew. It is interesting that Nineveh, where the Gilgamesh Epic was found, is less than 250 miles as the crow flies (or the raven, or the dove?) from Mt. Ararat.

There is no forest today on or near the slopes of Mt. Ararat, and there is no logical reason why there should be hand-worked wood anywhere near its summit. Yet we know that for at least four thousand years men have told of the flood, and of a boat, and of a mountain on which it came to rest. The general location of the mountain seems never to have been in doubt. It is logical, then, that for centuries, perhaps for millennia, the pious have made pilgrimages to the mountain which was holy. Did they perhaps carry the wood up the mountain to make shrines? Did early Christians build churches there?

The answer is not to be found on George Smith's clay tablets, or perhaps even in Fernand Navarra's wood fragments. In 1970 the SEARCH Foundation managed to raise more than $1 million, and to enlist the prestigious support of the Arctic Institute of

North America, the continent's foremost polar-research organization, to mount a truly scientific expedition to scale Ararat and search for the ark. Such support is not obtained just for the asking, and indicates a belief that there is something there. The scientists of the Arctic Institute drew up elaborate plans to drill into the "stagnant snow-ice mass" to determine the exact location and dimensions of what it tactfully called "the artifact," and then if possible to dig down to it, pump out slush, maybe even flood the icy mass with hot water to free it. Then, abruptly and dramatically, the Turkish government refused permission for the expedition to climb the mountain. No true explanation for the refusal was proffered, except "security reasons." Although eastern Turkey is still a military zone, ground security seems ridiculous in an era of U-2 spy planes and whirling satellites that can survey most of the earth—and do—without anyone down below ever noticing them.

Both SEARCH and the Arctic Institute have announced that they will keep trying. The chief of the expedition—British-born Ralph A. Lenton of the Arctic Institute, a man of impeccable credentials—said flatly that "There is something up there, something of great age and of unquestioned archaeological significance. Whatever is there should be uncovered."

If it turns out after all this time to be Noah's Ark, then it touched home just where it should have: in the land where legends come alive.

BIBLIOGRAPHY

GENERAL

Turkey. Life World Library, Time Inc., New York, 1965.

Ancient Civilizations and Ruins of Turkey by Ekrem Akurgal. Mobil Oil Turk A.S., Istanbul (English edition), 1969.

Turkey: A Traveler's Guide and History by Gwyn Williams. Transatlantic, Levittown, N.Y., 1967.

Aegean Turkey: An Archaeological Guide by George E. Bean. Ernest Benn, Ltd., London, 1966.

Anatolia I and *Anatolia II* (part of *Archaeologia Mundi* series). Nagel, Geneva, Paris, Munich (English edition), 1968.

ÇATAL HÜYÜK AND THE DORAK BUSINESS

The Dorak Affair by Kenneth Pearson and Patricia Connor. Atheneum, New York, 1968.

Çatal Hüyük by James Mellaart. Thames and Hudson, London, 1967.

THE HACILAR FORGERIES

Archaeometry, The Bulletin of the Research Laboratory for Archaeology and The History of Art, Oxford University, vol. 13, part 2, August 1971. The University Press, Cambridge, England.

279

BIBLIOGRAPHY

BIBLICAL TURKEY

The Bible Reader: An Interfaith Interpretation by Walter M. Abbott *et al.* Bruce Books, New York, 1969.

UNDERWATER ARCHAEOLOGY

Lost Ships by Peter Throckmorton. Atlantic–Little, Brown, Boston, 1963.

"THE GREAT CODE-BREAKERS"

Voices in Stone by Ernst Doblhofer. Kelley, Clifton, N.J., 1970.

TROY AND HEINRICH SCHLIEMANN

Gods, Graves and Scholars by C. W. Ceram, rev. ed. New York, Knopf, 1967.

INDEX

PHOTOGRAPH CREDITS

Ankara Archaeological Museum: pp. 161, 181. General Dynamics Corporation: p. 228. Ara Guler: pp. 101, 102, 103, 107, 113, 123, 162-163, 165, 193, 194, 195, 201, 218. Dora Jane Hamblin: pp. 16, 18, 25, 26, 32, 42, 44, 45, 46, 49, 52, 53, 54, 66, 69, 74, 82, 83, 91, 94, 95, 100, 102, 105, 106, 110, 111, 117, 126, 145, 147, 150, 151, 153, 198-199, 203, 206, 207, 208, 209, 211, 221, 232, 239, 240, 244, 245, 251, 254, 255, 262, 263, 264. John Libi: p. 268.